How Can
You Tell
If You're
Really
In Love?

How Can You Tell If You're Really In Love?

Sol Gordon, Ph.D.

Adams Media Corporation
Holbrook, Massachusetts

Published by
Adams Media Corporation
260 Center Street, Holbrook, MA 02343 U.S.A.
www.adamsmedia.com

ISBN: 1-58062-472-3

Printed in Canada.

J I H G F E D C B A

Library of Congress Cataloging-in-Publication Data

Gordon, Sol.
How can you tell if you're really in love? / by Sol Gordon.
        p.   cm.
ISBN 1-58062-472-3
1. Man-woman relationships. 2. Love. 3. Couples. I. Title.
        HQ801 .G5944   2001
        646.7'7--dc21   00-050417

This publication is designed to provide accurate and authoritative information
with regard to the subject matter covered. It is sold with the understanding that
the publisher is not engaged in rendering legal, accounting, or other professional
advice. If legal advice or other expert assistance is required, the services of a
competent professional person should be sought.

—From a *Declaration of Principles* jointly adopted by a Committee of the
American Bar Association and a Committee of Publishers and Associations

This book is available at quantity discounts for bulk purchases.
For information, call 1-800-872-5627

▪ Contents ▪

Contents

Contents

▪ Acknowledgments ▪

I am grateful to my editor and friend Rick Schultz, who patiently struggled with me while I was finding my own voice. He contributed his own voice to make a "finished" product that satisfied both of us. I am also grateful to the Adams Media freelance editor Erika Heilman, who added much substance to my book. My book is dedicated to my beloved wife Judith, who died in 1991—and to my dear friend Larry Bass, who died with three members of his family in a tragic automobile accident in January 2000. You are missed.

Perhaps it will mean something special to my readers to know that I still try to live fully.

So, the book is further dedicated to my new and loving partner Marlene Appley, my most influential friend Victoria Casella, and my best friend Peter Gollobin, as well as to the many unnamed voices that continue to enhance my life.

Sol Gordon

■ Introduction ■

Have you experienced disappointing love relationships in the past? Did you think the love you had
at one time would last forever? Do you suspect
that maybe you have never truly been in love?

This book is not only for single people who feel
something is missing in their lives, but also for
people who can't figure out why they bounce from
partner to partner. It's for people still hurt or puzzled
over a marriage that has fallen apart, or appears to be
heading in that direction. And, finally, it's about the
so-called "baggage" we each take with us into any
new relationship. Will we allow it to sabotage our
chances for a new and rewarding experience?

Whether you're single, married, divorced, or
have a history of failed relationships is not the
critical matter. What does matter is the active pursuit
of closeness with another person, and making the
effort to enrich your life through self-development.

Is it possible to find the love that's right for you?
Certainly it is. Yet a successful relationship isn't easy
to achieve, so don't despair if your initial efforts fail.

We are all subject to enormous cultural pressures that create unrealistically high expectations for our love relationships, making it especially difficult to find and keep love afloat. Many of us, for instance, have been deluded into thinking that *feeling* in love is all that matters. Advertisements, TV sitcoms, films, romance novels, and even some respected dramatic shows, for example, often recklessly exaggerate the significance of sex in a relationship.

However, as this book will demonstrate, the reality of lasting love partnerships stems from authentic *acts* of love. A love relationship remakes our world, giving it new life and meaning; being in love is loaded with potential. How the relationship turns out will largely depend on how well you know yourself and learning how to love another. In short, the give-and-take of relationships is liberating and self-fulfilling.

While this book celebrates love and recognizes that it represents the ultimate joy in life, its main purpose is to explore why so many people tend to fall in love with the wrong person. Given the high rate of infidelity, unsatisfying marriages, and divorce in the Western world, it's a simple fact that most people choose partners who are absolutely wrong for them. In addition, an extraordinarily large number of love affairs frequently end in disaster.

The title of this book, *How Can You Tell If You're Really In Love?* could be said another way: "How can I judge if the person I'm attracted to—or in love with—is right for me?" My goal is to help you answer that ever-important question. However, let's face it, when it comes to opportunities for finding the right partner, it's not always a level playing field. My basic approach is to remain optimistic. Indeed, one thing I've learned, based on many years of counseling single people who later found lasting partners, is that there's a potential someone for everyone.

As a clinical psychologist, I long ago discovered that not all relationship problems necessitate some form of psychotherapy to resolve. Frankly, the best "therapy" is finding the right partner in the first place.

Unlike many self-help books, you won't find a "quick fix" here. There are plenty of books and magazines that feature articles guaranteeing "Romance with Our Twelve Month Plan," or "Sensational Sex in Five Easy Lessons." These enticing offers for romantic fulfillment fan the flames of unrealistic fantasy rather than fostering authentic relationships.

My goal is to stimulate a rethinking of your existing ideas about love and the place of sex within a partnership. If this book elicits reactions such as, "I never thought of that before," "That's a good idea, I'll try it," or "That's a self-improvement area I need to explore further," then I've accomplished what I set out to do.

I'll also examine why many people put pressure on themselves and their current relationships by becoming preoccupied with past failures. Such barriers can be overcome. This book is an invitation to leave yourself open to love at any age, to help you decide whether your decision to commit to a relationship is rational and makes good sense for you.

Lasting love relationships are not the exclusive domain of married couples. They include marriages with or without children; gay or lesbian relationships; partners who live together; and, companionate relationships, where each person lives in separate dwellings or perhaps together in separate bedrooms. Some people might even decide that it's appropriate to maintain a single lifestyle supported by good friends. This book addresses those relationships as well.

Whatever your choice may be, there's one essential prerequisite for successfully discovering the right partner. In the stunning Indian film, *Dance of the Wind*, a renowned singer and preeminent interpreter of Indian folk music who is ill, conscientiously trains her daughter to take over her role after her death. When the mother dies, the daughter is scheduled to sing at her memorial concert. But the daughter, who for many years has lived in the shadow of her famous mother, cannot sing. Examinations show no medical problems. So the daughter goes on a journey to uncover the mystery. Eventually, she encounters her mother's guru, who tells her that she cannot sing in her mother's voice; she must find her *own* voice.

Like the daughter in *Dance of the Wind*, we must also learn to stay open to new ideas and experiences and not allow ourselves to be victimized by sometimes harsh and agonizing events from the past. By remaining hopeful about the possibility of change, and not getting hung up on comparing yourself to others, it is more likely that you will make wiser choices about love.

This book is about encouraging you to go on a journey of self-discovery—to find your own voice.

1

What Is Love?

We use the word love *in such a sloppy way that it can mean almost nothing or absolutely everything.*
—DIANE ACKERMAN

Love. It's one of the most confusing, imprecise, and demanding words in our language. What does it mean when someone says, "I love you"? Why do so many so-called "love" relationships fail? Was it really love that you felt, or was it something else? With a better knowledge of the different kinds of love and a fuller understanding of the many ways the word is used, you will be better able to separate immature love from mature love, fantasy and idealized love from energizing, responsible, and, most important, lasting love.

Let's begin with a concept of love by first considering sex. Many people confuse sex with love. There are people who have exciting sex and don't even like each other. Conversely, there are those who love each other but have uninspired sex lives. (By the way, about the dumbest thing anyone can do is to marry for sex. If sex is the only thing to look forward to in a marriage, don't marry at all. It's not worth it.)

If you consider that love, in addition to sexuality, can make one feel passionate, tentative, liberated, peaceful, and even frightened, it's no wonder why love gets so many people in trouble or creates extreme states of happiness.

People experience love in hundreds of ways, and it's impossible to predict how each relationship will turn out. No one can tell you what love is and how you should feel it. On the other hand, there are a few reliable time-tested predictors of good "love" relationships. For example, if your notion of love is based on, or tries to reenact, a romance novel, film, popular song, your parent's marriage, or is based on what someone else says is right for you, then it's likely to turn into a disaster.

There are many irrational standards for determining "true love." People talk about how "opposites attract," finding their "other half," and discovering their "soul mate." Some are convinced that they were lovers in a past life who have finally been reunited ("It was not an accident that we met"). These are no doubt deep and serious feelings, but when such vague and magical notions determine relationships, the results are rarely successful.

What harm can come if both lovers believe they were "meant for each other"? People in the rush of a new relationship often confuse intensity with love. They may incorrectly believe that love only happens once. Most of us realize that it's possible to feel intensely about, and even fall in love with, more than one person in a lifetime. The challenge, as always, is to fall in love and *stay* in love during all the changes that life brings.

In my experience over decades of counseling, couples that consider themselves "meant for each other" or who "fell madly in love" have often ended up separated, divorced, or in therapy. Their relationships have certainly not lasted as long as couples who married mainly because of each other's character, trustworthiness, and emotional stability.

Mature and Immature Love

To simplify the matter, love can be sorted into two categories: mature and immature love. Mature relationships are full of energy. You find the time to do almost everything you want to do. You are responsible. When you are with your partner, you enjoy each other. Sure, you'll argue once in a while, but you allow the spirit of compromise and a sense of humor to permeate your relationship. You want to please each other.

In an immature relationship, one partner repeatedly asks, "Do you love me? Do you really love me?" I advise the other person to say, "No." What follows may be the first real conversation in such a relationship. Immature partnerships are also characterized by promises to stop mean behavior. If a partner says, "Don't worry, honey, when we get married, I'll stop fooling around with other people," don't believe it. A bad situation is usually made worse by marriage.

How can you tell if what you're feeling is immature or mature love? In the first few months of a new relationship, you can't. Both kinds of love may appear and feel exactly the same. That's why I've often advised people, "If you feel like you're in love, you are." No one can know, in the early stages, if immature love will blossom into rewarding and lasting mature love. But after you settle into a relationship, all or some of the above-mentioned signs will soon appear. Then you will be able to tell if you are *really* in a mature love relationship.

A mature relationship is an evolving process, and not always an easy or magical one. Many partnerships, for example, start out with elements of immaturity, but become mature as a result of caring and effort. Some start out mature and become angry and hostile. The main point is that a mature relationship is always a work in progress. Sex and love are important, but not as important as having a partner who appreciates you and can be trusted. Fulfilling and lasting relationships are always about two people who are committed to each other's growth over a lifetime.

The Process of Mature Love

If we are going to create a more humane world, it's important to discover how to form sustained relationships that fulfill our deepest needs and contribute to an atmosphere of caring that the culture is crying for.

—HUGH DELEHANTY,
EDITOR OF THE *UTNE READER*

Love is a personal statement of the self and, therefore, does not lend itself easily to generalizations. Each person knows love in a unique way. We may love objects, trees, the sun, ballet, even books. Love for these inanimate things may be intellectual or aesthetic, but it is essentially one-sided and involves no interaction.

Loving another person involves elements of intellect, emotion, and activity. It is richest when voluntarily expressed. Loving your partner becomes more than the pleasure of just being together. It includes active concern for each other's emotional, physical, and material needs. It may be perceived as a responsibility, but seldom should feel like a burden, because you have consciously chosen to act in this way and are not merely reacting to the demands of your partner.

To love someone, you must also *like* that person. Often people in a relationship become unhappy when they are involved with someone they initially loved, but whose interests, and even mannerisms, become bothersome. The time spent together is exhausting in such cases, and the partners usually begin seeking diversions outside the relationship. Love creates its own balance—at times ecstatic, at other times boring. Most of the time, love lies somewhere comfortably in between.

What Is Love?

The process of mature love includes great risk. We let others know us when we speak honestly of our own feelings. Vulnerability accompanies self-disclosure. Taking the risk of being challenged on those points that are most sensitive to us suggests an openness and trust that is especially conducive to intimacy.

Love does not simply establish itself and then go on existing with no further care. Life changes and people change with it. Your own lifestyle and experiences, as well as those of the people you love, evolve at rates you cannot predict or control.

Myths and illusions continue to surround our concept of a traditional, loving marital relationship. For those influenced by the women's movement, however, marriage and marital love have become more realistic.

Women are no longer dependent on a husband for their economic success, status, or self-acceptance. For example, 60 percent of single women today own their own homes. And a *Time*/CNN poll revealed that 61 percent of single women, ages 18–49, said they would consider raising a child on their own. Women are more confident and self-sufficient than ever. They are also choosier when it comes to potential partners. They don't want to give up what they have accomplished. They want a marriage or partnership to add to their strengths, rather than detracting from their current, hard-won lifestyle.

While women may be choosier than ever, a recent *Time* cover story, "Who Needs a Husband?" (August 28, 2000), suggests that they are far from giving up on marriage. According to the article, only 8 percent of women (and men) do not plan to marry. About 80 percent of men and women still feel that they will find and marry their perfect partner.

Since fewer women are compliant, obsequious, or dependent, many men have had to rethink what they want in a committed relationship. Are they secure enough in themselves to handle a woman who has found her own voice? Of course, a male complaint is that some women are only interested in money and economic security. They have taken on the traditionally male breadwinner role to a fault. Indeed, as both men and women have found, people interested primarily in money often do not make very rewarding life partners. But men, too, are controlling in their own ways. Usually, this control takes the form of being uncommunicative or distant. Yet such counterproductive defensive strategies are often interchangeable: women can be just as emotionally unsupportive and uncommunicative as men. Like men, they can be supremely capable in the workplace, but emotionally adolescent—overly sensitive, defensive, and unrealistic—at home.

If relationships were easy, the divorce rate would not be so high. Yet the undeniable fact is that a more equal viewpoint strengthens a partnership, bringing with it a healthier and more lasting companionship. In fact, most relationship polls rate *companionship* over financial security, sex life, and the ability to have children. It is the glue, comprised of communication, trust, intimacy, and openness to change, among other things, that holds any worthwhile relationship together.

Some lament the passing of romantic illusions. A relationship can survive a few romantic illusions only if it is not based or dependent upon them for its survival. Since love cannot sustain the same intensity over time, there is a compelling need for two people to work together to get through the difficult times that will inevitably arise.

The process of mature love includes periods of indifference and animosity. The couple whose feelings do not change radically over the course of their life together is rare indeed. Many people marry with the notion that marriage will not substantially alter the texture of their relationship, a notion that is bound to be a source of major disappointment and frustration. Society, friends, and relatives all perceive people differently once they're married. Even couples who once thought marriage no more than "a piece of paper" discover afterward that the contract changed their expectations—of themselves, and of those around them.

Marriage, even when it lasts 50 years or more, unfolds as a combination of memorable episodes connected by the passage of uneventful time. Consider the things you enjoy most—sunsets, sex, your lover's smile, or any joyful occasion. How long do they last? Imagine how disillusioned you might be attempting to prolong unnaturally any of these events, which, though repeatable, are brief. The process of mature love accepts this fact of life.

The Ecstatic and Erratic Nature of Love

A life of feeling is bound to be a messy business. There's more fun to be found in the flux of things, grabbing what happiness you can, enduring what disappointments you must, than in pursuing an impossible ideal.

—RICHARD SCHICKEL

There's a reason why the difference between mature and immature love is indistinguishable during the first months of a new relationship. The symptoms of this ecstatic period—a pounding heart, trouble sleeping, a euphoric feeling—become a kind of alternate reality for a while as one focuses intensely on the other person.

Beyond this initial excitement stage, signs begin to emerge that help one differentiate between mature or immature love. For example, it's not unusual for people to realize that they are deeply in love with someone who doesn't return the feeling with equal commitment. Anyone may make a reasonable effort to evoke affection from another person. Sometimes this works, but if these efforts fail, a natural disappointment follows. Perhaps there's even a period of mourning for the failed love affair. After a time, however, people who are unable to abandon their one-way "relationship" may begin to appear tragically pathetic to their friends and families. There are few things worse than watching someone you care about try to force a person to love them.

The "Match Made in Heaven" Myth

One disturbing and pervasive myth says that there is only one true love on earth for each person. Thus, when a person's relationship ends, they may fear that they will never again experience the feelings of love they once enjoyed. Often, the opposite is the case: People tend to grow and mature through broken relationships. They often find that subsequent love relationships are more deeply rooted and emotionally satisfying.

Others repeat the same mistakes, continuing to fall in love with the wrong person. Why? One reason is that they consistently avoid introspection about the basic reasons for failure. Sometimes, of course, they may require counseling to help expose the real nature of the problem.

Building Self-Confidence in a Satisfying Relationship

There's a lot of good advice available about love and finding the right partner, but why are so many marriages, families, and relationships still falling apart? One reason, and a primary theme of this book, is that a lot of confusion arises from unrealistic expectations about what love can do for us as individuals.

Therefore, it's important, especially for people who have experienced the pain and disillusionment of unsatisfactory love affairs or disastrous marriages, to become aware of what constitutes satisfying relationships. In so doing, your self-confidence will increase, because you will realize that most of us *can* make good decisions in order to create lasting relationships.

Relationship Warning Signs

> *The whole notion of romance is based on not really knowing each other. That's why it's one of the first things that goes.*
> —SITA LOZOFF, CO-DIRECTOR
> KINDNESS FOUNDATION

Don't enter into a marriage or committed relationship merely because you are in love. Don't consummate a relationship without love or the potential for it.

Does this sound contradictory? It isn't if you realize that really being in love means taking the time, often months or years, to fully develop a relationship that is based on trust and a mutual desire to ensure each other's growth and development.

One Secret of Lasting Relationships

Another key factor in predicting the success of a mature relationship is the need for each person to feel secure. Are you confident you can function independently *without* a partner? If you want to know the secret of long and fulfilling relationships, that's certainly one of them. People who feel lucky in love most often cite "being able to do things together and apart" throughout their lengthy partnerships.

"My husband was never a great traveler," a friend, married for more than forty years, said. "He sometimes did it for me, but when I wanted to visit Ravenna, Italy, and take a mosaics class there for a week, I went with my friend. We had a wonderful time, and my husband was happy when he heard I had a good time. That's why I've always loved him so much. It was fun talking to him about what I learned in Italy, too. From time to time, doing things separate from each other really has enhanced our relationship over the many years. It makes us new to each other, for one thing, and our conversation keeps finding new areas of discovery."

There is no one prescription for a thriving relationship, and no "expert" can define for you what love means. But being able to function independently of your partner, and understanding what mutuality means, are keys to increasing your potential for living out a fulfilling and enriching love relationship.

■ 2 ■

Why Do So Many People Fall In Love With the Wrong Person?

The question to ask is not if I feel that I'm really in love but rather, is the love I feel the kind of love on which I can build a lasting relationship or marriage?

—IRA REISS

It's a fact that far too many people in the Western world fall in love with people who turn out to be wrong for them. According to a recent study, Americans are engaging in adultery at an alarmingly high rate. This statistic suggests that unhappy partners are looking elsewhere for what they are not getting in their current relationships.

The key question is: Why is "being in love" so often an unreliable indication of how a relationship eventually turns out?

I'm a big believer in love, and I'm certainly not against love's enchanting partner, romance. But, unless love emerges as a rational and life-enhancing force, the love you feel can make you miserable. After all, what is love? Among other things, it's an emotional state—potentially volatile, irrational, and blind—that often creates unrealistic perceptions and expectations of a partner.

That's why "being in love" should never be used as the only reason for making a decision about committing to a relationship.

Doubts about Love Are Expected

Here's an example of one attitude that discourages the possibility of a good relationship. It comes from teen idol, Ethan Embry, who said in *Teen* magazine, "Real love is more than a physical feeling." So far, so good. But, he adds, "If there's even the slightest doubt in your head about a guy, then forget about it. It's not real."

It's amazing how many adults share such an attitude, but unless the love you feel is a selfish fantasy or illusion, how is it possible not to have some doubts about a person? We have doubts about everything at one time or another. People are too complex to dismiss the possibility of love with such a cavalier attitude. Perhaps we can only quickly judge doubts about ourselves. However, it takes great knowledge about another person before we can understand whether our doubts about them are well founded or not.

How Do I Know If My Partner Is Wrong for Me?

There's no surefire way to know if someone is right for you. Only time will answer that question. Here's a case history of a person who was sure she had found Mr. Right after only a six-month romance.

■ ■ ■ ■ ■

Pam was 48 when she met Frank. She had been divorced for 10 years, with three adult children. Frank, 51, had been divorced for 12 years, with no children. It was "love at first sight." Both were health freaks, enjoyed excellent sex together, and experienced great times at movies, plays, etc. It was a classic case of "At last, we have found true love." It seemed like six months of heaven. Then they decided to go off on a one-month study tour of India. Suddenly, Frank, out of his element, became tense and edgy. Pam loved the experience, but Frank was bored and started smoking again. As the days dragged on, they both saw that their interests were very different—even their politics were at odds. Their revealed values became the subject of continual arguments. They broke up. Both were depressed and disappointed. They had looked forward to this kind of trip, believing that it was going to be the beginning of an ideal life together.

■　■　■　■　■

The case of Pam and Frank is fairly representative of couples who bring high expectations to a relationship before they have allowed enough time to really get to know each other.

What Are Some Signs That a Partner Is Wrong for You?

In the early stages of a relationship, there are some surefire signs that a partner is wrong for you. Watch out for a partner who:

- Lies a lot
- Has multiple excuses for coming late, or forgetting dates
- Seems distracted, instead of paying attention to you
- Initially tells you he (or she) is not married, but you discover he (or she) is
- Has serious lapses of attention, forgetting birthdays or other special occasions
- Is preoccupied with his (her) own needs
- Doesn't return your phone calls; instead, he (she) offers lame excuses
- More than once is physically or verbally abusive, even if they apologize or say they were "just kidding"

All of the above can still be in the context of a relationship that offers hot sex and good times. However, relationships that exhibit these warning signs rarely last.

Deciding to Stay or to Let Go

Deciding to stay in or to let go of a relationship is hard, largely because many people feel insecure about finding another one. They feel doomed, that this is their last chance. Others feel that this is all they can get, or all they deserve. Such behavior is based on low self-esteem. In abusive relationships, a person might feel they deserve what they're getting. They blame themselves, or they feel if they're patient enough and offer enough love, they can get the relationship to work.

Generally, people who have found their own voice don't stay in bad or abusive relationships.

Confused about Love

Marriage is difficult enough without bringing low expectations into it.
—*SLEEPLESS IN SEATTLE*

Do you remember the nice guy, played by Bill Pullman, who is dumped by Meg Ryan for a total stranger (well, he's Tom Hanks) in the hit movie *Sleepless in Seattle*? Is he ever lucky to have gotten out of that engagement! His comment about bringing "low expectations" into a marriage is perceptive, but the real problem usually has to do with expecting too much, or expecting all the wrong things. If the film continued after the couple finally meets at the end, the Ryan and Hanks relationship would probably fall apart quickly. It's easy to imagine either character, as presented, eventually saying in disappointment "You're not what I expected, now that I know you."

Here's a similar real-life case from the pages of Abigail Van Buren, one that offers a warning to readers. "Dear Abby" replied to a letter from a distraught unmarried mother who was worried about marrying a man she clearly respected, but about whom she wrote uncertainly, "I don't think I love him." Abby told her to forget about him, adding: "…Marriage is supposed to last forever and that is a long time to feel like you've sold out."

I responded by writing "Dear Abby" the following letter, taking serious exception to her ill-considered reply to "For Better or Worse" ("She's Engaged, but Her Heart's Not in It."):

> Your response, "Let him go," to a confused 29-year-old, unmarried woman with a nine-year-old daughter was wrong headed. After describing her hard

working boyfriend as an "ideal husband," the correspondent worried that she wasn't "in love" with him.

So many marriages that begin with "love" don't last. Often, people find love only after a relationship has been tried and tested. Maybe that's why so many people who start off madly in love soon end up just mad.

We all have strange ideas about what love is, and we sometimes don't realize that what really counts in a relationship is trust, caring, and a commitment to each other's growth. Perhaps that's why so many marriages built on "being in love" fail.

I'm not opposed to love however it's defined. But was it smart to advise a woman to "let go" of someone she describes as a "wonderful man" she's been seeing for "more than two years"? That sounds like a good working relationship, for her and her child. More serious, you may have reinforced in her mind an essentially adolescent, self-destructive ideal few of us ever find—or would want to find.

> We all need to know the crucial
> differences between feeling in love, true
> and responsible love, and compatibility.

In the original letter to "Dear Abby," "For Better or Worse" suggests a degree of uncertainty by wondering if she's read too many romance novels. Perhaps she has. In any case, it's a common enough dilemma. A large number of people are so influenced by Hollywood-type images of love and passion that they feel disappointed if they're not "dancing on clouds." If they are not dazzled, then how can it be love?

In her very perceptive book, *Swept Away* (1984), Carol Cassell observed: "Women can—and do—make their entire lives unhappy and unfulfilled because of this insistence on the perfect Slayer of Dragons, the one-and-only rescuer." Of course, men also do this, perhaps looking for the perfect *Sports Illustrated* swimsuit model-type, or "cute" and "adorable" (read: easily controlled and non-threatening) fantasy girl-woman.

Give love a chance to triumph over fantasy. See if love develops, especially if you really like someone. However, don't dismiss the fact that some people marry because of fears concerning loneliness and security. Sometimes, even such poor reasons can start good people on the path to a true and fulfilling partnership based on love. Why not commit on the basis of appreciation and caring? Maybe the woman who wrote "Dear Abby" did not take her advice and is happily married and in love with her "wonderful man."

Blind Love

> DORA: You know how most people fall into one or two groups. . . . The couples who stay together because they don't believe they can do better, or the lonely, miserable people who live alone, but then there's this microscopically, teeny group of lucky people who get to be with the person they're madly in love with.
>
> PAUL: Dora, you ever consider being "in love" and leaving out the "madly" part?
>
> DORA: What fun is that?
> —FROM *LOSER*, A SCREENPLAY
> BY AMY HECKERLING

For some people, love will always—compulsively and impulsively—remain a thrill ride. There are those who simply enjoy the ups and downs of short-term, intense relationships. Like the character in the above passage from the screenplay *Loser*, they perceive being swept away as the only avenue to experiencing a love relationship.

I'm not giving anything away by revealing that Dora is in a doomed relationship, exploited by an older man who does not respect her. Still, she lives under the delusion that eventually he will reward her devotion with love. Paul's advice to Dora (leave out the "madly" part of being "in love") is astute. Only by seeing herself and her lover rationally and clearly will Dora have a chance for a true and lasting love partnership.

Destructive Cycles: Falling In and Out of Love

Why do some people fall in and out of love? The pattern is a familiar one. Initially, there's a period of great love and excitement that leads quickly to disillusionment. There's truth to the observation that people who fall easily in love fall easily out of it. Repetitive patterns of moving from one relationship to another may reflect an underlying fear or anxiety concerning intimacy. After all, brief relationships often do not allow intimacy, which takes time and trust to develop.

There are other reasons why destructive cycles repeat themselves. It's not unusual to encounter individuals who are so desperate for love that they're willing to take all kinds of risks to get it. Thus, their own self-worth and happiness may yield to the powerful need to be attached, whatever the cost. Peer pressure, or an ingrained attitude that going out with someone is always better than being alone on Saturday night, can seduce people into making unwise decisions in their choice of partners.

Another common destructive cycle can occur when love is confused with sexual gratification. Both men and women sometimes use sex to relieve intolerable feelings of anxiety. This may create a temporary illusion of love.

Love Disaster Predictors

If any of the following applies to a relationship, its potential for failure will be that much greater:

- When myths, illusions, unreasonable expectations, and false assumptions weigh heavily in a relationship
- If one or both lovers are neurotic, character disordered, self-centered, sexually perverse,

on an ego trip, power hungry, or just plain disrespectful and mean

- When love is like an addiction: possessive, madly and effusively romantic, or full of anxious despair ("I know she doesn't love me, but I'm desperately in love with her," or "I'll go crazy without him.")

Keep in mind that even healthy love relationships can involve brief periods of panic, vanity, a need for reassurance, craziness, hostility, and boredom. However, when emotional or physical abuse is involved, they should be of immediate concern. You may be in love with the wrong person.

The Myth: Four Stages of Love

One conventional view of love relationships is that they go through four distinct stages:

1. Infatuation
2. Romance (in love)
3. Deepening affection
4. Commitment (mature love)

It's a "tidy paradigm," these four stages—too tidy for me.

Loving someone involves more stages than most of us usually recognize, not just those that can be categorized into these four progressive phases of love. It involves learning about each other's temperaments, making compromises, perhaps juggling careers or tackling parenthood. It involves rites of passage that a couple will share over time—births, deaths, aging. That's what makes a lasting love relationship so complex— and ultimately so rewarding.

Destructive "Love" Relationships

Many of us are at least acquainted with examples of false, destructive "love" expressed in anger and violence, or as emotional or physical abuse.

- "If you leave me, I'll kill you."
- "If you reject me, I'll kill myself."

A client revealed the following: "I dearly love my wife, but these days I can't stand the sight of her. At times, I want to kill her with my bare hands." Another said, "I love my wife so much, she belongs to me. If she so much as looks at another man, I will kill them both." That last remark eerily duplicated O. J. Simpson's admission to a reporter for *Esquire* magazine, "Let's say I committed this crime. Even if I did this—it would have to be because I love her very much, right?"

Unfortunately, many of us have probably heard people say, "If you are not jealous, you are not in love." *The Jerry Springer Show*, for instance, thrives on presenting dysfunctional couples who appear to believe such destructive notions. In a typical program, a man betrays his wife with another woman, even fathering a child with her. He says he does not want to return to his wife. After they try to beat each other up on nationwide TV, Jerry asks the wife why she wants her husband back. She replies, "I still love him."

Daytime television is preoccupied with love and sex in soap operas. These shows are watched by millions of viewers and feature episodes of infidelity, suicide, violence, murder, betrayal, and rape. Yet, somehow "love" is twisted into every one of these horrible activities.

Sex is often equated with love, but so is jealousy. Neither should be seen as proof of love.

Jealousy

I'm not referring to jealousy as the playful kidding around that sometimes occurs in a good relationship. I'm talking about neurotic jealousy, in which suspicion, resentment, and envy become corrosive. Take a look at the word itself. The last part spells L-O-U-S-Y for a reason. Jealousy always brings misery with it. It's a hidden or conscious desire to control the impulses and behavior of the other person. Jealous men and women wish to control their partner. Sometimes, it is masked in the language of love ("It's because I love you so much that I don't want you seeing him again"). The suffocating exclusivity demanded by jealousy kills any chance for personal growth or true love.

In this regard, it pays to clearly communicate to your new partner the nature of your former relationships. Will you still occasionally be seeing each other because you have remained friends? Do children enter into the picture? If so, one would hope this means that there will be some valuable and continued contact with the ex-partner. It's important that, prior to marriage, your new partner understands and appreciates the role your ex may continue to play in your life.

Cultural Pressures

Romance and Sex: The Quick Fix

If TV conditions us to expect too much, or many of the wrong things, in relationships, then magazines sell the fantasy of the quick fix. *Cosmopolitan* and other mass women's magazines offer articles on the best ways to have an orgasm with your partner, or the sexiest places to make love. One such magazine features the quick fix of "27 Signs You're in Love." Almost all of the 27 signs were frivolous: "You check with your horoscope to see if he's right for you"; "You stop watching the news"; "When he's not with you, you sleep in his underwear." Articles such as these are meant to entertain, not necessarily to intelligently or helpfully inform.

In another magazine, there's an article about how a man's nose, eyes, and mouth can reveal—in six seconds!—his love potential. Still another magazine predicts, "Soon there may be a medicine for couples to enhance love." The height of silliness emerges in newspapers and magazines around Valentine's Day. For example, an article in an issue of the *San Francisco Chronicle* in February, 1999 states that "When our pheromone cloud bumps up against another person's pheromone cloud . . . Our clouds want to mingle and form an even bigger and better cloud or they want to float away . . . A whiff of the person's pheromones snap your vomeronasal organ into action . . . If yes, stay near this person, get closer. Fall in love or lust with this person. If not, get away as soon as you can."

Everywhere we turn, we're faced with glamorized, idealized versions of love. It's as if the culture wants us to stay trapped in the fantasy and does everything possible to encourage and expand that fantasy...

—FLORENCE FALK,
NEW YORK CITY PSYCHOTHERAPIST

For many individuals, a striking gap exists between the public image of love and their personal history of it. Since Hollywood images usually depict love as sensational and glamorous, they do not even remotely resemble most people's private experience. Thus, feelings of inadequacy and internal conflicts can develop. Why does my relationship seem so boring when compared to what everyone else seems to have? This type of imagery is something many people simply have to get over when they become adults.

Therefore, examine your ideas about romance and love. Are they creating problems for you by being unrealistic? Are they creating unfair and unjust expectations from imperfect but loving human beings who may indeed be right for you, given the chance? Romance is like water. We all need it in our lives. But, it makes sense to strive for a balance in your life: Allow reality to enhance your notion of romance. That way, a deeply loving relationship will have a chance to develop into a lasting one.

If life is often not like the media images portray it to be, neither are the lives of the actors all glamour and romance. More than one movie star—Tom Cruise and Nicole Kidman, Tom Hanks and Rita Wilson, Susan Sarandon and Tim Robbins—has talked about picking up their kids from school, doing homework with them, and helping with the cooking and other chores around the house. Their real lives turn out to be made of the same stuff that all of us experience. On the one hand, this realization might shatter the illusion you've had of a movie star's life. On the other hand, however, seeing these lives full of the joy and satisfaction that comes from enriching relationships with a partner and children is a tonic. It means that their so-called "glamorous" lives are potentially attainable by all of us.

> *Trying to forge an authentic relationship amidst all the romantic hype makes what is already a tough proposition even harder. What's unique about our culture is our feverish devotion to the belief that romantic love and marriage should be synonymous.*
> —Florence Falk

· 3 ·

Durable Relationships

A Lasting Love That Developed Slowly

The world of marriage and love partnerships is a various and wide one. Are there any secrets to be revealed about those "lucky in love"? See for yourself. Here are a few examples of relationships that continue to grow and thrive.

■ ■ ■ ■ ■

The background

Eric is a strikingly handsome man. He's athletic, very social, and a high-level computer expert. He and his friends (most of them male) go off on fishing, hiking, mountain climbing, and biking adventures. Before he met Susan, he had few dates and no hot romances. After graduate school, he traveled around the world by himself. He made friends wherever he went.

Susan, an architect, is good-looking but not gorgeous. She's athletic and loves to travel and read. Susan also has many friends. Unlike Eric, she dates whenever she can and has had several promising romances that didn't pan out.

The meeting
They meet by accident at a professional conference; both are 28 years old. They recall having a pleasant conversation, but neither felt their meeting would emerge as a possible romance. Eric takes her phone number anyway. Three weeks later, his work took him to her hometown and he called her. They met and had an enjoyable time. Their common interests—athletics, travel, a liberal political outlook—made for lively conversation and future possibilities.

Romance develops
Three months later, after occasional dates, they began considering the possibility that they were

having a romance, even though sex had not entered the picture yet. Though they really liked each other, neither was consciously in love.

Love considered

After another three months pass—more nights out, sex, fun times vacationing together—they decide (independently) that maybe they are in love. They decide to live together to see how things will work on a daily basis. It works!

Ten years later

Now, 10 years later, after marriage and two children, they both acknowledge that their love for each other developed very slowly. I asked each of them separately the secret of their successful marriage. Each called the other partner a "best friend." They both said that their relationship is joyful and intellectually stimulating. They both enjoyed sex, but emphasized the importance of almost daily intimacy—touching, kisses, and kind words—in their marriage. They each pointed to being able to have friends separately and together, without jealousy. Two or three times a year, Eric travels with his friends, and Susan visits her family with the children. They both added how much they respect each other's community-mindedness regarding the volunteer work they do.

Eric and Susan are the happiest married couple I know.

■ ■ ■ ■ ■

More Secrets about Durable Relationships

There are many ways of looking at relationships. Helena Amran, a well-known and apparently successful matchmaker based in Israel, suggested that in her experience, "The only durable matches are those in which one of the partners is very much in love, and the other learns, over time, to return this love." However, this is simply one model for marriage. No longer does marriage come in one form—of a leader and follower, or of a dominant man and submissive woman, for that matter. Modern marriage comes in many forms, four of which we'll consider next.

Four Marriages

1. Overcoming Fear of Marriage

Ralph had an ongoing relationship with Rena, a colleague at a large university. They did not see each other during working hours. She liked him but would only commit to the occasional sleepover. Neither dated other people. Ralph was crazy about her. He did everything he could to please her. I sensed that Rena even intimidated him a bit.

Alone one day, she decided to take a walk to a nearby historical site. She sat down on a stone wall when a stranger came over and started a pleasant conversation. His name was Jack. He was an architect and new in town. They were married four years later. Why was she able to work through her fear of marriage with Jack and not Ralph? Who can say? This time, however, she cared enough about him to make it work.

Jack and Rena are still going strong after three years. Isn't it romantic? Yes, but her hang-up about marriage was severe. The *un*romantic fact is that Rena and Jack went to counseling for two years before they actually got married. It was the realistic, *not* the romantic part of their relationship, that taught them they could trust enough to commit to each other.

2. Culture Shock: Arranged Marriages

A couple I know from Calcutta, India view Americans as silly and absolutely obsessed over the concept of love and finding a "dream partner." Their story would make most of us run for the door.

When Roshan was 12 and Sarita was seven, their parents promised them to each other. He came to the United States when he was 18, went to college and earned his Ph.D. by the time he was 26. While he was not celibate during this time, he respected his parents' wishes concerning his marriage partner. He sent a letter to Sarita's parents asking that she be sent to America. They would marry shortly after her arrival. They had not seen each other for eight years. Alas, her parents refused to send their unmarried daughter to him. After much negotiation, they married by proxy. But even that tactic failed to bring them together. Roshan then spent a full year dealing with the red tape of Immigration Services, trying to prove that Sarita was indeed his wife.

By the time she arrived in New York, it had been almost 10 years since they had last seen each other. Roshan told me this story six years after his marriage. By then, he was the father of three children. Both of them were very happy with the marriage and the life they were building. They were never nervous about marrying, nor were there any romantic notions involved. They simply loved each other very much and decided to work at their marriage—and it worked!

We cannot change what our culture teaches us from birth, but Roshan and Sarita's story should make us pause and think about why and how we love.

3. The Manly Man as Tender and Caring: Managing Role Assignments

My friend and colleague, Larry Hopp, enjoys a marvelous marriage with Muriel. I asked him to comment on his view of the role of men and women in a relationship.

One facet of our relationship I found amusing was that I was probably more of a feminist than Muriel. Understandably, her life experiences suggested a woman's/wife's role nearly opposite to my perceptions. This sometimes was problematic since Muriel could not easily accept that a man could be sensitive, warm, loving, caring, and still be "manly"! Tenderness from a man was not something she had experienced, although she recognized that these were characteristics she preferred. There were no household chores offensive to my sensibilities. My masculinity was never threatened by performing "female" tasks as opposed to "male" tasks. I also felt strongly that as a father I wanted to play a significant role in the rearing of our children. There would not be any conflicts as to role assignments.

An important distinction had to be made between dependent and independent needs. We were both feisty enough to want to be independent while still needing each other. Anticipating and meeting the needs of the other became a hallmark of our relationship. We didn't wait until the need was so obvious that it would, or could, become dangerous. We listened carefully to vocal tones. We watched body language. We developed a sensitivity to all kinds of signs and signals from each other.

4. A Marriage of Two Minds (and Bodies)

Joe and Pat are a childless couple who have been living in reasonable harmony for 23 years. Overall, they are still happy together. Here's how they see their successful relationship.

After the initial attraction, their decision to commit was based on an agreed-upon understanding of what makes for an enduring partnership. Growth—individual and together as a couple— was a major goal. For them, mutuality was a key to whatever happiness they would share together. Indeed, they share common values and some, but not all, interests. They settle inevitable arguments by saying how they *feel* rather than what they think. The use of "I" messages is standard in their home.

Joe takes care of all financial matters. Pat prepares most of the meals and enjoys gourmet dishes. Pat also does most of the driving because Joe isn't as good behind the wheel. Each of them wanted to share in the other's special talents. They agreed long ago to teach each other what they know, without being patronizing in the process. They agreed that both of them had to know how to keep functioning in the event that one of them was away, ill, or if one of them died.

They manage their own private time. They share some friendships, but also have their own close friends. They see their partnership as a journey. If it doesn't work out, they feel their relationship would remain strong enough to sustain a continuing friendship. With such positive and strong family values and attitudes, it's unlikely that

Pat and Joe will ever break up. Incidentally, Joe and Pat are a gay couple.

To sum up, these four stories about committed relationships reflect vastly different life experiences. From the way these couples met to how they developed special traits together, they are all unique. Their lives together encompass the characteristics they brought to, and developed within, the setting of their particular partnership. For this reason, we can never look to anyone else's relationship and wish ours were like theirs. It's like trying to change our fingerprints or DNA. Whatever our partnership turns out to be, it will not be like anyone else's.

There is no destination on the life journey. Living it fully brings us opportunities for change and growth.

▪ 4 ▪

When Is the Best Time to Commit to Someone?

It's true that the intensity, the emotional high that comes with loving passionately (or foolishly) often sustains even the worst relationships—for a time. But this passionate and exciting initial or early stage of love is also unreliable. In the best of scenarios, love settles into a sober, rational, but no less rewarding passionate partnership. *This* is the time to make the decision whether or not to commit to a relationship!

Over the years, I've noticed that many people resist this idea. Perhaps it seems too analytical and unromantic. Experts often make distinctions between immature and mature love—between infatuation, romance, and commitment, for example. But do these insights make any difference to the people they describe? Sometimes, but not always. That's why it's important to acknowledge that if someone says he's in love, he is. Who are we to say it isn't love?

On the other hand, if someone is truly looking for a relationship that will stand the test of time, what is the alternative? In our culture, one alternative has been called "serial monogamy," which means jumping from partner to partner. When the mystery and intensity of romance wears off, these people typically move on to someone else. This is a flight from love—a flight from creating a passionate partnership, over time, that is based on true and mature love.

Why Are So Many. Mistakes Made in the Name of Love?

There are hundreds of theories about the causes of confusion over love, the influences that may cloud our view of it. These are most commonly dished out:

1. Hollywood-style romantic films
2. MTV
3. Romance novels
4. Family pressures

5. Cultural imperatives
6. Astrological signs
7. Money
8. Status
9. Chemistry
10. Love at first sight

Such influences bombard our everyday thinking about love. But even if every theory offers a glimmer of truth, they offer small comfort to people who do not wait for the rational period of love to settle in before making crucial decisions. Inevitably, there will be some people who are so inflexible and so limited by character disorders that a rational period of love never happens to them. We all know, or have known, people who keep making the same mistakes over and over again.

Aside from the cultural forces conditioning us as to what to want and how to behave, several psychological pressures also contribute to mistakes made in the name of love, such as feelings of inferiority, desperation, loneliness, unworthiness, and unrealistic expectations.

Other forces at work include people close to us who send out confusing messages. Typical remarks many of us have heard at one time or another include:

- "He's not right for you."
- "She's only after your money."
- "But your partner isn't [fill in religious faith]."
- "You two are the perfect couple."
- "Isn't 15 years a big age difference? What's your partner going to look like when you're 50?"

And, lastly,

- "I don't know how to tell you this, but your partner fools around a lot."

Many of these above-mentioned pressures and mistakes can be handled and avoided by:

- Giving a relationship time to develop
- Discussing critical issues at length with your partner
- Taking important issues seriously enough (physical, emotional, or drug abuse; irresponsibility; respect and trust)

Questions to Ask Yourself about a Potential Partner

In keeping with the idea of choosing your partner with a rational frame of mind, it's important to ask yourself a number of questions about your potential partner. Consider the following:

1. Does the love I feel for this person enhance my ability to be a good partner, mother, or father?

2. Have I considered how unreliable sex is—and even the notion of love itself—as an indicator of a relationship's potential to last?

3. Do I know my partner enough, and like my partner enough, to work through periods of disappointment and unmet expectations regarding love and sex?

4. How important are romantic images of love or hot images of passionate sex to you? Could you commit to a relationship based, for the most part, on reality?

It's okay to be somewhat unsure and insecure about the answers to these questions. All of us can be viewed as works in progress, and the answers could change over time.

Can Love Conquer All?—Constructive Relationships

I have seen successful marriages and committed relationships that conform to no norm and standard. There are a lot of studies, theories, generalizations, stereotypes, and prejudices about love, but someone who may be right for you is a real person, not a statistic or type. So, yes, sometimes love does conquer all.

- There's Phil, married to Janice, 17 years Phil's senior. She has three adult children close to Phil's age. I've rarely seen a more loving and joyful couple.
- There's John, a self-described bisexual, who loves his heterosexual wife. She knew about his bisexuality before they married. They now have two adorable children, and their marriage is more stable than most "normal" heterosexual couples I know.
- There's short, plump, and brilliant Sarah, who is older than her tall, rugged husband, Matt. They are living happily with their three children on a kibbutz in Israel.
- There's Arlene, a powerful businesswoman and her househusband, Norman, who cares for their two small children. He's been

described as "effeminate," but they have great sex and adore each other.

These may be exceptions to the rule, but I could cite many other examples of "different" couples who are happy with each other. My own marriage can only be considered "different." We were married for 38 years. My late wife, Judith, was a professional, caring, and popular social worker who was a wonderful cook and mechanic. She did all the so-called "male" things around the house. I helped with the dishes and childcare. She was a much better driver than her distracted-at-the-wheel husband. She also had a tremendous gift for languages. I sought fame and attention, traveling extensively, lecturing, and, often with Judith, writing books. She didn't fuss about my being away a lot. We enjoyed our frequent vacations together, and she had a best friend who was her safety net. We loved each other.

Despite the unfortunately high statistics about failed marriages, all the jokes aimed at married couples, and all the people who say, "I don't know of a single married couple who is happy," there are millions of satisfied couples who have been together for nearly a lifetime and are happy with their lives. They even get along with their children!

I can't think of a better arrangement—and here I include any truly committed and loving relationship between two people—even with all the potential pitfalls and problems.

Creative Fidelity

Can monogamous relationships last? Can they remain interesting and exciting? It helps when each partner is free to go off for a day or evening with a friend—male or female—without guilt, suspicion, resentment, or jealousy. This healthy attitude can enhance relationships. That's one way you and your partner can construct a framework for creative fidelity. We need to be reminded that fidelity need not be boring. It can be a continual striving to enrich your relationship through ongoing trust.

Love Decisions

It's difficult to make clearheaded choices when we are most in love. Love, after all, is such a joyful state, which is why we all look for it—even when we may already have it! But, that's another story. Many of us know people who realized too late what they had. They sacrifice the real lasting thing for the short-lived fantasy.

Be aware of these factors in your relationship decision-making:

- Cultural influences, such as films, TV, ads, magazines (Are you letting the seductive romantic period of your relationship sucker you into not seeing how uncaring and irresponsible your partner is?)
- Social and economic forces (Are you being swayed by your friends or parents to marry too soon or for the wrong reasons?)
- The mystery of "attraction," or so-called "pure chemistry" (Are you just throwing the dice, hoping that good sex and feelings of neediness will lead to a long and rewarding partnership?)

The Myth of Having to Love Yourself First

Can you love someone else if you don't love yourself? Of course it's easier to establish a relationship with another person if you have a high level of self-esteem. Many people, however, are deprived by parents who do not love them, or who have a severe inability to constructively express their love. This is especially true of men who were deprived of any affection or intimacy from their fathers.

As a result, when these children reach adulthood, they cannot easily receive or give love to another person. It's no accident that many seek relief from these feelings of being unloved and isolated by becoming addicted to drugs or alcohol. Some also give up on love by becoming workaholics, self-defeating perfectionists, or by feeling dominated by a vague sense of unworthiness. Therefore, giving too much credibility to the idea that you have to love yourself first dooms millions of people to a life of despair and desperation.

The fact is that people do respond when they are loved or cared for by others. They also respond well when they are pushed, or luck into, situations where they are appreciated. For instance, some Twelve Step programs and group encounters give people who are initially afflicted by feelings of self-hatred a start in turning their lives around.

One technique, for example, is when people who don't *feel* worthy of love expand their mode of behavior by *acting* as if they do. It's like the old AA expression, "Fake it until you can make it." Other effective ideas: Start by directing some activity toward others; volunteer time to help disadvantaged children (if that issue is too intense, then devote time and effort to another area of social concern).

Actions change you, and your good actions change you for the better. See if you don't believe yourself to be more lovable once you think less about yourself and more about others. Loving is indeed a strange and wonderful paradox!

Some Relationship Stereotypes Are from Mars, Others Are from Venus

> *Treat a man like he's a creature from another planet, and he'll act like a creature from another planet.*
> —STEVEN CARTER AND JULIA SOKOL,
> *MEN LIKE WOMEN WHO
> LIKE THEMSELVES*

Are there natural differences between men and women? If so, then love can only flourish when you respect these differences. My own view, however, is that cultural and societal forces determine the main behavioral and psychological differences between men and women, especially how our parents have raised us. Therefore, these forces can be reshaped and changed.

Many of us have been exposed to simplistic ideas of compromise regarding the maintaining of relationships that are not likely to have been sound in the first place. Married partners, for example, often attempt to stay together to preserve family unity. For the sake of the children, the couple will develop all kinds of compromises to stay married. Such arrangements do not necessarily make a good marriage, or bring happiness to anyone. On the other hand, sometimes a compromise can be good, because the end result might be far better than the consequences of a disastrous divorce.

There are stereotypical notions about those who act "just like a woman" or "just like a man." These views are a kind of avoidance, often representing ways of covering up basic personality flaws. In an egalitarian partnership, differences between the sexes enhance, rather than detract, from the relationship.

Beware of such stereotypes. It is not helpful to avoid addressing crucial issues by saying "men are like this" or "women are like that." A resignation, which is a kind of despair, can set in, and it becomes all too easy to give up on trying to change a bad situation. It is much better to operate in terms of conflict resolution, while remembering that not all conflicts need to be resolved. Some tension and differences of opinion exist even in the best relationships.

The best approach is to find legitimate, workable compromises that satisfy both partners in a relationship. Don't expect to solve every problem. As philosopher William James observed, "Wisdom is learning what to overlook."

Imago, or . . . Why Is My Partner Just Like My Mother/Father?

"Imago" is a fancy version of the word "image," coined by psychologist Harville Hendrix. One example: "My girlfriend is so domineering that she wants to control every situation in my life—just like my mother tried to do." Thus, the concept refers to how we may unconsciously choose a mate, who, along with having attractive qualities, embodies the very negative and destructive traits of our parents that "wounded" us as children.

This compulsion, first suggested by Freud, is toward identifying with aspects of the living or deceased parent that are embodied in our selected partner. The compulsion generally gathers its steam from the parent with whom we experienced the most unresolved conflict. Perhaps, unconsciously, we feel that now we can finally make things "right" with our troubled partner, who will eventually reward us—as our own parent did not—with praise or unconditional love. That rarely happens, however. Instead, a destructive cycle of behavior is more likely to continue.

Of course, it would be simple to warn, "Don't choose a partner who resembles an abusive parent." But people do it. Even the great actress Katharine Hepburn did it, throughout her life remaining hopelessly devoted to an alcoholic lover, Spencer Tracy, whose hurtful behavior mirrored her own abusive and distant father.

Be aware of this limited but useful theory, and be armed against this often destructive, sometimes tragic, tendency. Once we are educated about this possibility, we can recognize when a partner resembles an abusive parent, and then avoid him or her like the plague. Also, be careful how you apply anyone's theory to your life. Theories can be made to "fit" almost any situation. That doesn't mean they are true.

· 5 ·

How Do I Know If
I'm Really In Love?

*Love is an ideal thing, marriage is a real
thing: a confusion of the real with the
ideal never goes unpunished.*

—J. W. VON GOETHE

How do I know if I'm really in love?
That's a question all of us have asked at least once
in our lives. It can be a source of confusion
throughout even a long and successful relationship. Recently, a man told me he'd been on a business trip for two weeks, away from his wife. "I
didn't think I missed her," he worried. "Does that
mean I don't love her anymore?" After a bit of
conversation, it was clear that it meant he had

grown comfortable and trusting enough of his partner not to fret unnecessarily. That's the pleasure—the sanity—of a good relationship. He realized he'd certainly have missed her if he came home to an empty house. So here's a guy with a good relationship and he's still scratching his head over it!

What about the rest of us who presently have no one waiting at home? How will we know when love has struck? One answer sounds naïve, but it's accurate: If you feel yourself to be in love, then you are. The problem with this "feeling" is that it's too often not enough to rely on to make a rational judgment, or it is misleading. Many therapists, for example, hear about the "gorgeous-looking," "ideal" partner whose charm turned out to be a screen hiding a physically and emotionally abusive personality.

If you're reading this book, you have probably already experienced what it is like to fall in love with someone who was not right for you. Most people, if the high divorce and adultery rate is any indication, fall in love with the wrong person. Perhaps the love affair ended as a big disappointment. Worse, maybe it ended as a terrible trauma or tragedy whose burden you are still carrying.

So let's look at this very important question again. This time, we'll focus on the word "really"— as in "How can you tell if you're *really* in love?" What's actually being asked is, "How do I know if the person I'm in love with is good for me?"

Never has this question been more crucial as a predictor of a potentially lasting relationship. We live in strange times where "cyber affairs"— dating over the Internet—has led to the ruin of many relationships, and the beginning of many more. With this technology, however, comes the hard fact that it's even more difficult to get a grip on the actual person we're dating. For one thing, it's just too easy to engage in creative lying on the Internet. For another, many of us realize that talking to a stranger is often easier than talking to our partner or spouse. So the illusion of intimacy can quickly be established over e-mail.

We'll discuss the consequences of this modern development and some cyber dating etiquette at greater length later. For now, let's get back to the question at hand. Since all-consuming, sweeping passion diminishes over time, and often for good and acceptable reasons, what of love survives? If you are in, or about to embark on a new relationship, ask yourself these questions.

A Love Checklist

Have I reasonably concluded that the person I love:

1. Can be trusted?
2. Seems also to love me?
3. Would make a good parent, if we decide to have or adopt children?
4. Is loyal?
5. Could be moody and have some problems, but is basically kind and compassionate?
6. Respects me?
7. Can handle inevitable conflicts as they arise with maturity and considered action?
8. Has control over the volatile and often destructive emotion of anger?

These are key questions. Inevitably, they can be relationship deal breakers. Moreover, you can know the answer to them only over time. That's why the early stages of being in love are so tricky.

Now, the "Feeling-in-Love" Questionnaire

Let's now take a look at a list that's a surefire way to meet a partner and have a short and unrewarding relationship. This list is one that many people itemize, like a grocery list, knocking out any place for an actual human being with its high expectations and idealizations.

I must have a partner who is:

1. Sensitive and has blue eyes
2. Devastatingly beautiful
3. Dark-haired
4. Blonde
5. Big-breasted
6. Muscular
7. A fan of the film *An Affair to Remember*
8. A fan of the movie *The Dirty Dozen*
9. Great in the sack
10. Tall
11. Rich

Notice that none of these attributes go to the core of a person's character. They don't let you know what you will actually have a year down the road. Your tall, rich, blond partner may have a terrible problem with anger, or have no desire to discuss problems with you. This is a recipe for disappointment and disillusionment. In the heat of romance, you may fall for the exact opposite of your compatible partner. Instead of a caring partner you can grow with, you might get the one that merely looks good, or the ill-considered one of your dreams. And that's where the partner may eventually return—to your dreams. You'll have the wrapping and not the real flesh-and-blood package.

Don't Make Any Crucial Decisions ... Yet

The main thing to keep in mind about the being-in-love stage with a new partner is that it's *not* the time to make a decision about a committed relationship. It is a highly unrealistic time, one in which you have a deceptive state of mind. When decisions are made in the height of passion, they frequently turn out to be mistaken or wrong, sometimes leading to bitter disillusionment.

So, though it may *feel* right to act impulsively, keep in mind that time is your friend in making sure this partner is the right one for you. True, there are many marriages that started out as impulsive and passionate ones, and they last because they eventually grow to allow compromise and change. But some methods are more like throwing the dice than others. Indeed, too many of these impulsively committed relationships end in separation and divorce. One reason: It's simply too difficult to sustain such a high-flying union. When the passion and energy diminishes, so does the relationship.

How Can I Tell If a Love Affair Is Moving in the Wrong Direction?

Warning Signs

Consider the following warning signs of a relationship that's potentially headed for failure:

- When you're tired a lot of the time
- When you can't stand being with—or without—the love partner
- When you find you are becoming mean or unkind to friends or family
- When you are easily irritated, but still feel in love
- When the romantic excitement makes you feel nervous
- When the romance exerts a disorganizing or chaotic effect on your life

How Will I Feel When I'm Really in Love?

In contrast to the energy drain that accompanies immature love, mature love is more steady, rational, and dependable. Possibly, this is because it's somewhat less passionate, but not necessarily! When real love takes hold, amazing things can happen:

- Both of you will experience high levels of energy for everything you want to do.
- Your work and important tasks will not be neglected.
- You will feel kind to each other, and most everybody else.
- You will discover your life priorities.

There's another aspect to a healthy relationship. Satisfied couples are committed to working out ways to resolve their differences.

One True Thing about Love
In all my years of counseling couples, I've found one thing that remains absolutely and consistently true about mature love: Kindness and energy informs and elevates the lives of people who are *really* in love.

These views about mature love closely parallel the thoughts of contemporary Buddhist philosophies, such as those put forth in *The Art of*

Happiness by His Holiness the Dalai Lama and Howard C. Cutler. Don't worry about whether you share their religious views, because their insights about love are very rewarding. In Buddhism, the primary meaning of love is friendship, compassion, and the joy that comes from kindness. What they call "true love" brings joy to ourselves and the loved one, as well as the people we influence. It involves respect, patience, and tolerance.

What If You Are Not Sure You're In Love?

Very often I've heard people say, "I met a person who seems just right for me, and who I find attractive, but I don't feel the chemistry. Where's the high, the excitement that everybody else talks about and that I'm supposed to feel?"

Generally, there are several "buts" involved in the question. "We have a good time together, but she's taller than I am." "I love his sense of humor, but he's a bit overweight." Or, an age difference of several years is mentioned. The feeling amounts to this: "I'm not sure I'm in love." This uncertainty is a serious one, and it often leads to a partner prematurely breaking off a relationship.

Given that we're exposed to so many contradictory messages about what love is supposed to be, no wonder people are confused. Here are a few questions to consider if you are uncertain about a relationship:

- So what if love didn't strike you like a bolt of lightening?
- So what if it wasn't love at first sight?
- So what if you're not yet sure about the relationship?

If your partner seems right and is good to you, why not risk staying in the relationship for a while? Why not take a much longer time to make a decision to commit? As I've discovered over the years, love often develops over time for many unsure couples. After all, where is it written that you must only commit to someone who, from the first meeting, made you weak in the knees?

In my experience, the "unsure it's love" couple stands a better chance of developing an ongoing, wonderful relationship than the impulsive, "madly in love" couple. After several months of marriage or living together, many "madly in love" partners become just plain mad.

Why Should I Compromise?

In discussing this issue with a group of young single adults, most of them disagreed with the above advice. Why? Because they felt that to continue a relationship without feeling intensely in love would be the height of hypocrisy. It would surely mean making a terrible compromise. The best part of a relationship for them was the excitement, vitality, and joy of being in love.

That's great, but what if the "right" person does not come along under these very favorably passionate circumstances? How many people will miss out because they were not patient enough to see if love—even the intense kind—might emerge later?

Is Mutual Attraction the Key?

No, but make no mistake—mutual attraction is wonderful. In many cases, it's a prerequisite for continuing a relationship. Attraction alone, however, is not enough to successfully sustain an ongoing relationship. Ayala M. Pines expresses this well: "No matter how powerful the attraction, no matter how unique the chemistry, no matter how promising the potential, getting to know another human being is a process that can't be rushed."

Who Is Right for You?

The first step toward answering this question is to learn more about how you feel. That will help you to determine whom you really want for your life partner. Examine what is happening to your own body. Is it "alive" or "dead"? Does it feel energized, hurt, or plain exhausted? Again, keep in mind one key to your behavior. Are you kind and relatively calm, or are you mean, nervous, and irritable? The heart is often deceptive, but the body rarely lies.

· 6 ·

Learning to Choose a Healthy Relationship

Exploring Missed Opportunities and False Perceptions

Common sense tells us that when two people first meet, they would be wacky to expect their relationship to last forever. But sometimes that's exactly what happens. Sometimes, two people are ready to take a chance and make a shift in their lives. Change is all around us, in society and within ourselves. There is always the possibility of a new relationship—if we are open and ready for it.

Understanding a Modern Relationship

If only finding a lasting relationship were as easy as reading a book on the subject or going to a fortune-teller. Let's face it, though, no one discovers a life partner that way. Hundreds of books have tried to uncover what makes us tick in a relationship. Still, we don't understand enough. If we did, the divorce rate would not be running neck and neck with the rate of marriage.

Perhaps our expectations about the nature of relationships have changed dramatically. We need only look at what we expect from marriage today as compared to the past. It doesn't take much thinking to realize that without equality and freedom of choice, a relationship in today's faster paced society would be ineffectual and unworkable over a long period of time. No enlightened person would want to go back to the period of arranged marriages, which usually meant loveless unions that could not be dissolved. (I should note here that for some religious groups, however, arranged marriages are still the norm and seem to work for them.) Nor would we want to return to a time when women were not allowed to vote or inherit property. Today, people benefit enormously from finding mates who can be equal partners in love, family, and society.

We sometimes need to be reminded how far we have come, and the importance we now place on love and caring in relationships. Most people believe that both men and women should be happy in their unions—a radical idea not prevalent in all cultures. Some partners, however, are clearly not happy but choose to stay together anyway. These choices are often influenced by strong belief and value systems.

It's great that our choice of partner is not the result of a business decision made by our parents or society. Making a choice about a life partner, however, is harder than ever. It's more problematic when so many people admit they are too busy to give a relationship the time and attention it deserves. Ironically, when I speak to such people individually, they inevitably say that forming a partnership and living one's life with another person is at the top of their list as the most meaningful of human experiences.

The Perfect Partner in Our Minds

So, as I've mentioned, many relationships that seem to start off well unravel within a short time. Why? One reason is that they are based on something we've made up. Many people tend to make choices about who they will love long before they actually meet that person. For example, someone may only want to have relationships with others of their own race, religion, educational level, etc. For others, physical attributes play a big part in defining their partner choices. Height, body shape, eye color, and even the way someone smiles may be very important. We contrive our own "perfect partner" in our minds. For some, this picture can become so compelling and refined that they won't even think about dating a person who does not fit their rigid profile.

When potential partners are approached with so narrow a focus, it is no wonder so many excellent opportunities go unnoticed. More important, we are more likely to choose the wrong partner with these strict attribute lists as our guide. Within such a self-defeating framework, there's no room to find out if a relaxation of the profile might have brought the desired relationship into our lives. Furthermore, some people are so in love with their own abstract notions of a love partner that they often fail to see the real thing when it's right in front of them.

To be sure, we must like something about a person's physical presence. As I argue throughout this book, however, character and personality traits always prove much more important in a long-term relationship than any given physical attribute. A partner can look like a movie star, but is he or she reliable, caring, funny, charming? Physical characteristics, also, inevitably change over time—that lean build you admire may thicken, your lover's full mane of hair may thin and turn gray.

If you fall into this self-defeating category, start by finding some clarity on the subject of who would be your best partner. Name those things that are most important to you. Think of positive attributes, such as honesty, trust, faithfulness, a sense of humor, and generosity. Look for those qualities in a person that go beyond the physical.

Creating False Limitations

■ ■ ■ ■ ■

Sonya is 48, divorced, with two grown sons. She's a well-established physician with a good income. She is pleasant, attractive, affable, and very bright. Sonya was eager to find a marriage partner, but had been having bad luck. "I'm giving up on men," she told me. "All they want is sex. I like sex.

There's no trouble with my libido. When I date a man, he will always be the type that turns me on. But what I'm looking for is a man with whom I can have an intelligent conversation. More than anything else—even more than sex—I want to have a mental orgasm."

Three weeks later, she told me that she had found her dream man. He was handsome, a real turn-on for her. He was also a scholar who was independently wealthy and crazy about her. Ah, if only that were the happy end of the story. It turns out there was one catch for Sonya: he was 10 years younger. "I've already told him I can't see him anymore," she said. "I can't handle the age difference."

I couldn't believe she was serious. I told her to relax and enjoy the relationship for a while and see how it might develop over time—that she should refrain from projecting or speculating on what the future might bring. Nothing worked. She dropped him cold.

Sonya needs to work on her perception of age. Many 48-year-old women would love to have such a wonderful man come into their lives, regardless of his age. Perhaps she did not recognize the power of the active and curious intellect to keep a person young. She probably did not see that she looked and acted much younger than her 48 years. Sonya got stuck on the idea of "What will other people—my friends—think?"

■ ■ ■ ■ ■

Changing Your Perceptions: Allowing for Reality

One way to get closer to actual reality, rather than misperceived reality, would be to listen very intently to your conversations with others. Do you feel your conversations are colored by your beliefs about particular subjects? Listen carefully and critically to yourself. Question your own words. Listen to the way you tell stories about daily activities or people you see. Is there a tendency to exaggerate or inflate details in your telling? How do your perceptions of reality color your words? Are you always the underdog—the poor person to whom something pernicious is being done? Is there an element of anger or vehemence in the stories that you tell about what happened at work or on a date? Check to see if your responses to daily life are distorted or inappropriate. It's crucial to be aware of how they affect your relationship to others.

Partners with Disabilities

False perceptions also color our view of people with disabilities. When we talk about potential partners, how many of us are open to the idea of meeting and falling in love with someone who is blind or in a wheelchair or otherwise disabled? If it's true that a person's values, personality, and character are important in a relationship, then why are many people uncomfortable when they first meet someone with a physical disability?

This is an experience common to us all, but it's not one that should stop us from getting to know a person. One gets beyond physical differences quickly. Sure, some disabled people are mean and bitter; others are delightful to be around. In short, they are just like everyone else.

The disability is not a primary determining factor as to whether someone is, or is not, a good candidate for partnership. It's the personality of the individual that counts. To be sure, physical accommodations need to be made, but they can usually be managed without too much trouble.

Ask yourself, "If I married a person who was in an accident and, as a result, was confined to a wheelchair or possibly disfigured, would I desert him or her?" "Would I stop loving someone because of a change in appearance?" I certainly hope not. If they withdrew from you, and your relationship did not improve after giving it your best effort, separation would be an option. But suppose they continued to be as loving and considerate as they had before the accident or disease. Would you leave?

> *If I made a mistake, I've got to forgive myself for being human. I'm in the process of doing that now.*
> —CHRISTOPHER REEVE, *STILL ME*

The actor Christopher Reeve is a prime example of what I mean. Since his horseback riding accident, which left him totally paralyzed, he has shown great courage and determination. He is truly a magnificent human being. He continues to work at his craft as an actor and director. His family has stayed together. No one can know the torment they had to endure to get to this point. He and his wife, Dana, and their children, make me proud to be part of the human race. His friends, who have been faithful and supportive, are *true* friends. We can all be very sorry that he had such a tragic accident, but the grace and courage that have resulted from that terrible moment in 1995 are not to be denied.

Are All Good Men Married or Gay?

■ ■ ■ ■ ■

Like Sonya, Susan is another lost cause. She's 35, has been divorced for eight years, and has two young children. She's an attractive teacher, with an ex-husband who provides adequate support for the children. She told me that all the good men are either married or gay, and all the others were either too macho or sexual perverts. Then she met her "dream man"—a never married 40-year-old who adores her and the children. She described him as a rich man with a terrific personality and marvelous sense of humor. She said he was "great in bed."

What could be wrong with such a guy? Susan found something. He was short—shorter than she is. She was ashamed to introduce him to her friends. As diplomatically as possible, I told her she was nuts. That was not what she wanted to hear, so she terminated her therapy with me.

She broke off the all-too-brief relationship. Will Susan be happier with a tall man who dislikes her kids and needs her income to live on? What if he's grumpy and humorless, but tall? Will she be happy? Probably not. Susan is another case of someone allowing limited perceptions—of herself and others—to ruin a potentially wonderful relationship before it has a chance.

■ ■ ■ ■ ■

Be Honest with Yourself

Anybody possessing analytical knowledge recognizes the fact that the world is full of actions performed by people exclusively to their detriment and without perceptible advantage, although their eyes were open.
—THEODOR REIK

Only we can figure out what is most important to us. We must be able to trust our good judgment, and our gut, to make the right decisions. This may sound like a simple thing to do, but it's not. Most of us have a hard time being honest with ourselves. We are convinced that the reason we are not happy with our life, or have not found the relationship we want, is outside our power. In truth, we have the power to make our own heaven or hell—to create the circumstances to change things in our lives for the better. It has always been a mystery to me why some people turn potential happiness away when it knocks on their door. On the other hand, this may be one reason why I've never been unemployed.

People with a good sense of who they are formulate images of themselves and their potential partners from their own value system. They do not rely on the advice of family or friends about how they should feel or what kind of person would suit them best. While the questions and concerns of those who care about us are always valuable tools in helping us make important decisions, they cannot be taken as our truth.

We've all heard the phrase "Perception is everything." We all use our perceptions to form judgments or rationales about the world. We think our perceptions are objective reality—the Truth— and we rarely question them. One of our biases might manifest itself as optimism, not a bad quality to have. But we might be so optimistic that it clouds our judgment. We've all known people in sinking relationships who say that everything is okay, even after many bad signs have been revealed to us.

Misperceptions often cause unnecessary misery, and are harder to recognize.

■ ■ ■ ■ ■

Not long ago, Joan and her husband, Tom, were out having a drink when Tom's former girlfriend, Laurie, came up and started talking. As Joan saw it, Laurie was flirting with Tom while ignoring her. It didn't matter that Joan and Tom had been married for 15 years. Joan's anger started to boil up.

Tom didn't think that Laurie's behavior was out of line. As he perceived it, the situation was merely a brief chat with someone he used to know and hadn't seen in years. The reality probably lay somewhere between what Joan saw and what Tom saw. We don't know what Laurie was thinking. But Joan's perception was off the scale. If reality had been a player in this, Joan would have said something cute to her husband, such as "Glad to see you still have it, honey." Tom would have felt good about himself and the matter would have been forgotten. But, no, the arguing went on for days, with poor Joan suffering and needing a lot of reassurance from her husband.

For Joan, it was real. She would not—could not—concede that her perception of the situation was strongly colored by something inside herself that had nothing to do with objective reality. In therapy, I'm hoping she will learn to question her thinking, leading her to be more conscious of negative and inappropriate thought patterns. In time, she may learn to look at situations more objectively. Both Joan and Tom will be happier if she achieves some control over her distorted perceptions.

■ ■ ■ ■ ■

Stereotyping Potential Partners

Stereotyping potential partners is another way we limit our field of opportunity, thereby increasing our chances of picking the wrong partner. By stereotyping people, we quickly accept or dismiss them. It's a reductive behavior that demeans a potential partner as well as oneself. If you fall into this habit, consider how you would feel if grouped with everyone else in terms of, say, sex, race, religion, hair or eye color, political party, or intelligence. Meeting an attractive man or woman, and then casually dismissing him or her because you dislike his or her profession or politics often turns out to be grossly unjust. That kind of stereotyping causes us to miss opportunities, diminishing us in the process.

In their refreshingly clear-eyed look at male-female relations, *Men Like Women Who Like Themselves*, Steven Carter and Julia Sokol observe that negative male stereotypes only function as "obstacles to intimacy." The same is true for negative female stereotypes.

A Personal Checklist

Behavior such as stereotyping people often reflects a person's insecurity and sense of inferiority. This is a good time to take a personal inventory. What don't you like about yourself? Are there parts of your personality that would not be—or have not been—constructive and nurturing in a relationship? In counseling, people have often found it useful to work on their negative personality traits. If you have 10 things you could work on, choose one for now. The effort will show immediately. We always have the ability to change ourselves for the better. Don't squander the opportunity. In going into your next relationship with the hope that this time it will be a rewarding and lasting one, you can address those negative behaviors that have caused trouble—for you and your partner—in the past.

Listening Skills

One negative and all-too-common trait is exhibited when one person compulsively monopolizes a conversation. This bad habit sometimes reflects a need to control and always reflects a lack of skill in being able to give and take in a relationship. It may also simply be initial nervousness with a new person. All the while you are chattering away, you may be anxiously thinking: "Does she like me?" "Does he think I look okay?" "Does she think I'm a jerk?" "Why can't I shut up?"

Those who tend to dominate conversations, however, never seem to realize how others tune them out. When someone takes over a conversation, it becomes very hard to listen. This is a good way to spoil a date before it even gets started. None of us deserves this type of treatment from a potential partner.

In this regard, women and men want the same thing: to be listened to. If your partner is a good listener, and you are a good talker, be sure you also know how to reverse roles. Listening skills are sexy, and there's a lot to share in "getting to know you" conversations. Just be aware that you are the most interesting person you know—but only in your *own* mind.

Listen to what is being said. You can't listen well if you are constantly trying to think up something bright and witty to say. Some big talkers miss important things that the other person has to say, such as "My big desire in life is to move to New Zealand," "I'm leaving my dental practice to travel the world," or "I'm saving my money for plastic surgery because I'm unsatisfied with how I look." It's possible these facts, if heard, could influence your decision whether or not to see this person again.

If someone is overly competitive, even on a date, and needs to play one-upmanship in conversations, you need to decide if you find it irritating, or just a minor flaw among other great characteristics. It's worth finding out.

Pressure to Commit

By far the most difficult part of making the decision to commit to a relationship is listening to your own voice. I've mentioned reasons why people may initially choose the wrong person unknowingly, but what about when someone realizes they have chosen the wrong partner—and marries that person anyway?

Unfortunately, it happens all too often. People go through with a deal they know will not work out. Men and women get caught up in being with each other, being with friends, and telling people they have finally found the right person. Almost before they know it, they're planning to move in together or to get married. In these situations, the *promises* become the driving force, leaving little time to spend on the most important question of all: Is this relationship right for me?

Throughout my long career, I have heard people say, "I knew he was not the right person, but I just couldn't seem to stop the progression of events." Or, "Before I knew it, I was saying 'I do,' but in my heart I knew I wasn't sure at all." And, "I felt like my fingers were crossed when I promised to love, honor, and cherish and all that stuff." If you recall any of these lines from your own first disappointment in love, read on.

Knowing When to Hesitate

A short time ago, a friend in her 40s sent out wedding invitations. Ten days before the ceremony, all the invited guests received a note saying that the wedding had been postponed indefinitely. My first thought was, "This is a smart couple." They were wise enough to put everything on hold until they could work through their difficulties and uncertainties. Perhaps they will still marry someday. It was clear, though, that they were strong enough not to compromise their future for the sake of a ceremony and some guests.

Sometimes the person who has doubts might have to stand alone—in opposition to a partner who may be sure of his or her commitment. Then there's the added pressure that two families and all your friends might bring to bear on the situation. In any case, such uncertainty must be respected. Whether it's due to fear of responsibility or doubts about the chosen partner, waiting is preferable to making a life-long promise that you may not be able to keep.

While loving partnerships should always be embraced with eagerness and joy, it pays to be supportive of a couple who expresses—either individually or together—serious doubts. Indeed, if an unsure person feels pressured into a commitment, they may sabotage the relationship and any hope it might have had to succeed.

Other Negative Traits

Suspicion and confusion grow out of lies. Many people I have counseled deal with issues of trust in their relationships. We must be able to trust our partner. Otherwise, we may become anxious about many seemingly trivial things: "Where's the money

I left on the dresser?," "Was Bill really 'out with the boys'?," "Why did it take Debbie three hours to go grocery shopping? What's she hiding?" When lies enter a partnership, we become unsure of each other. Life becomes a jigsaw puzzle where even simple conversations become fraught with anxiety, leaving us feeling off-balance. It is an energy-draining process.

What can you do? Pay attention to the words you use. Say what you mean. If you have a habit of lying, consider that it may be a defense mechanism due to being unsure of yourself. It takes determination to monitor what you say to people, but the freedom you will experience in being yourself becomes its own reward. Becoming a genuine person is a very attractive quality.

In learning to tell the truth, be aware of the *way* you tell it. There's truth that is meant to hurt another: "Your shirt doesn't fit you anymore, and you look awful." Or, there's truth that's told out of hostility: "I don't care if you shower five times a day, you still smell bad." This is just plain mean. Truth and kindness need not be strangers. Try those sentences above this way: "I prefer the blue shirt you wore last week." Or, "Honey, maybe you should see a doctor. That odor might be due to some kind of health problem."

Sometimes people lie because they judge that others are not strong enough to hear the truth. This occurs quite often within families. Relatives judge what is okay to say and what is not. This sets up a situation where collusion among different family members comes into play. Be sure you are not trying to control or patronize the other person. You will know how to handle such predicaments if you ask yourself some of the following questions:

- How would I like to be treated in the same situation?
- What's the worst thing that can happen as a result of telling the truth?
- Could the truth lead to a dialogue that will clear the air?
- What is so fragile about the other person that makes lying preferable?

Be very careful you are not making unfair judgments out of your own fears.

Acting Like It's Love: Spotting Problem Behavior Early

Many people fall in love with someone who is not right for them. Why? Could they have spotted disturbing behavior at the start and done something about it? Most of us bring to a relationship some aspects of our own distress, fears, phobias, obsessions, and unrealistic expectations. But when does a problem really become a *problem*?

A partner's behavior is often masked in the early stages of romance by great sex, wonderful vacations, gourmet dinners . . . you get the picture. Not much of the problem behavior is likely to emerge at that time. It's rare that a couple gets to know each other during the early stages of falling in love. It still could be love, because friends see it as love, it feels like love, and both partners act like they're in love. Mostly, the good times don't last uninterrupted by conflicts, arguments, disappointments, and even breakups. It's during these times that a relationship can be tested to the benefit of both partners. First, discover if you got into the relationship to avoid or get away from yourself. Did you go into it to lose or find yourself? In conflict situations, you have an opportunity to get in touch with yourself and still maintain your integrity. What we often learn about ourselves in a conflict situation is not always flattering. Instead of asking what we can learn about ourselves, more often we try to get our partner to change. Disagreements can become a key element of growth.

Not every issue warrants attention. Sometimes it's appropriate to compromise or give in. There is folk wisdom that says, "If you are right, say nothing; but if you are wrong, apologize." We learn less about ourselves during harmonious times than when we need to resolve a problematic situation.

If only it were easy to avoid the wrong people! But when they are charismatic and fun to be with, that isn't always possible. Often, people in destructive relationships say that Ms. or Mr. Wrong brings an intensity to their orderly and sedate lives that is otherwise absent. These relationships cause enormous damage over a long period. That's because, typically, a partner only gives up on changing the troubled person after enduring much abuse and emotional chaos. As I have seen many times, people caught in such destructive relationship cycles literally have to be forced to give up the abusive loved one.

■ ■ ■ ■ ■

In the case of Brenda, it took her 10 years to finally break off her relationship to Frank. "I separated from him many times, and tried several other relationships. These partners were kind and pleasant but extremely boring," she said. "I kept going back to him because of the excitement, but he was never really interested in me as a seriously committed, or marital, partner. I was just a good-looking sex toy he could show off, but he was never nice to me in private."

This is a sad story told over and over again. It's one in which there's no likelihood of any enduring or genuine partnership ever occurring.

■ ■ ■ ■ ■

After a Breakup

Consider the following suggestions if you find that you have recently gone through a breakup:

- Don't immediately move into a new relationship.
- Don't tell everybody about it.
- Talk to one or two good friends.
- Ask what they think went wrong.
- To everyone else, fake it, if possible; most people don't care about your problems.

- Don't be surprised by these rude and unhelpful responses: "You think you've got problems? Wait until I tell you mine." And the ever popular, "You'll get over it; we all do."
- Listen carefully.
- Don't get angry if someone says, "I knew it all along. I didn't tell you because I didn't feel you could handle it."
- Meditate.
- Relax with massage.
- Volunteer your time; it is a healing process.
- Exercise, even if you hate exercising.
- Take a daily, hour-long walk.

Our Disposable Society

There is no "human nature" but only changing notions of [people] depending on the changes in society.

—J. H. VAN DEN BERG,
A HISTORICAL PSYCHOLOGY

Because ours is a wasteful, consumer-oriented society, we may be unaware how it can affect us in our personal relationships. We can easily become desensitized to the vast differences between people and things. If a partner changes in some way, or offers you a constructive challenge or confrontation, are you more likely to get defensive and begin thinking of moving on to another relationship? I've seen many people who do not think about fixing a situation. Instead, they just want to be rid of it, like just another disposable good or fast food item.

This attitude is deadly to love. Face the reality of your situation, rather than turning away from it. Rational thinking and compromise allows for growth. Perceptions are destructive because too often they provide *insufficient information* to work with. They may be merely mental contrivances, used to rationalize or "prove" our "case." Too many people give up too easily on new partners, allowing false perceptions ("He's a controlling type," or "She's just after my money") to keep them romantically challenged and alone.

· 7 ·

Are You Single by Choice or by Bad Dating Habits?

Many people may be surprised when they discover that this is a question not so easily answered. For example, we may not be aware how we act with a new partner, and since dating is a stressful as well as an exciting time, our behavior may be affecting our chances with desirable partners. Similarly, our expectations about a new partner may be obstructing and limiting our chances of having a successful relationship.

Some unmarried or long-unattached men who enter middle age are likely to start asking themselves one question: "Why?" They begin to suspect that something other than "unavailable partners" is the source of such a consistent lack of success in this area. Indeed, there are plenty of single men and women out there also looking for partners. So why are many men who want a long-term relationship having such trouble connecting with a partner?

Generally, men who claim to have "high standards" in terms of superficial outward aspects, like beauty, or who look for much younger partners, have the most trouble. Consider the following stories.

■ ■ ■ ■ ■

Max and Robert are both somewhat overweight and are not particularly good looking, especially by TV or magazine-model standards. That is, they are like most people out there in the dating wilderness: great guys, once you get to know them. Both men, in their 40s, are capable, intelligent, and have energy and imagination.

While Max has amazing success with women, Robert does not. Here's why.

Robert approaches women on the basis that *he* is attracted to them. The potential partner, however, has no knowledge about him. "When I go to a single's dance, I zero-in on the most beautiful woman there," Robert says proudly. No wonder he's always shot down! His approach is aggressive and intrusive. Could Tom Cruise get away with this risky technique? Sure, but we're not talking about Tom here.

Max, on the other hand, makes a point of never approaching someone until he has somehow made himself known as a competent, knowledgeable, and interesting guy. Since women are given a chance to know Max first, he has had no difficulty relating to as many women as he desires.

There is a problem, though. Max, unlike the never-married Robert, is divorced with three adult children. He is cautious about starting another deep involvement. Ironically, his sensitive approach has resulted in several women falling in love with him.

Since he's a client, I know firsthand that he hasn't fully understood the consequences of his actions. "But I tell the women that I'm not ready for a full commitment," he protests. The fact that he's charming and funny, and that he has sex with them, should alert Max to this simple point. His partners go by who he is and by what he *does*, not by what he says. Inevitably, there's a painful breakup over a relationship that *he* never wanted in the first place, but that she understandably fell into.

■ ■ ■ ■ ■

For Women: Relationship Alert!

Perhaps I should call this the "Max Alert." After all, many women will know this guy at some point in their lives. So, be alert and sensitive. Don't allow such things as seductive talk and sex to hide issues that may be crucial to you. For example, listen to a partner when he says, "I don't want a committed relationship. I just want to date and have good times with you." Take it literally. Don't think you will change him. It rarely happens. If you continue the relationship anyway, at least you will be doing it on equal terms.

Are You Inviting Rejection?

Let's return to Robert, who wants a long-term relationship, but always manages to find himself single. By being so preoccupied with his own ego-gratification, he almost invites rejection. For one thing, his tendency to select the most attractive and desirable younger woman at a single's dance or group event signals an extreme insecurity about his own body image. Inevitably, he is rejected, since there's no outwardly physical reason for a stranger to find him immediately attractive or desirable. Like most men, he simply cannot compete on that level, nor should he want to; he's merely setting himself up for failure.

Establish Yourself As an Interesting Person First

Have you ever noticed how some people who remain unaffected by their age, attractiveness, or desirability become very attractive to others? When someone gives a talk, for instance, it doesn't matter how the speaker looks. Inevitably, many people will gather around that person later. (I recall how hundreds of people—mostly women—would line up to hug Leo Buscaglia after a talk.) In such cases, the audience now knows a bit about how the speaker sees the world and feels about things.

That's just one example of how revealing some of your inner life—not all at once, and not everything, but a glimpse of it—can often act like a magnet. It's the same principle for one-on-one relationships. For most people, that simply means allowing time for someone to get to know us before we "zero-in" on that ideal stranger.

Where's Robert Today?

So far, Robert has had little or no short-term (three or four months) success with women. He remains single at 47, but has decided to channel his energy, at least for now, into his creative work. He's put dating on the back burner. Meanwhile, he recently joined a nondenominational church where he sometimes leads discussion groups. My guess is that he will eventually meet and find a potentially lasting relationship through this group. Certainly, it offers a friendly context in which people can get to know him by experiencing his most attractive qualities: a good sense of humor, questing spirit for knowledge, and an engaging warmth and energetic drive.

Meeting Strangers:
The Pressure to Jump into Commitment Again

We have examined a common situation among dating men, one that can apply equally to women. Many of us, for instance, have known recently divorced women who "shoot too high" when they return to the dating world. When they are rejected, depression, made worse by the recent divorce, often sets in.

■ ▓ ■ ▓ ■

Joy and Pamela are two recently divorced women who handled their divorces in different ways. When new relationships didn't work out quickly, Joy remained open. She did not become desperate. She continued to be comfortable when friends introduced her to men. She found private dinner parties to be an effective meeting place. A dog lover, Joy also met interesting single men with puppy in tow.

Socially comfortable, Joy made friends of both sexes. She was not in a hurry to get remarried. She did not feel pressured to have sex right away with a new partner, or to date only one person. Indeed, her comfort and openness to social occasions was largely due to not being dependent on meeting and dating a man.

Friends First

At social events, Joy would talk about her two children to new friends. She was open about her life. As a result, when she made friends with men and women, she seemed to make the right kind of friends. That is, Joy's patience and honesty about her life became an attractive and endearing quality about her. No wonder she met someone! Joy and her partner became friends first, and now consider marriage a real possibility.

Too Fast, Too Soon

Pamela took a different avenue. After her divorce, she charged into the dating ritual and found herself having many sexual relationships. A few months later, she was disillusioned and depressed. Her calls to men she had slept with were not returned. Pamela's life went into a tailspin of depression. Suddenly, there were no dates, no sex. Pamela had no energy for either!

Luckily, she had several supportive friends, who advised her to date again. Her work, however, consumed all of her remaining energy. "Besides," she told her friends, "Who has the time to date?" Her level of distress was too high. But she realized that watching TV every night exhausted rather than energized her. So she decided to check out Internet dating services and connected to several men. Initially, it acted as relief from boredom and despair, but it soon rekindled her interest in dating.

After three months of fooling around with a number of men on the Internet, she agreed to meet one of them. Encouraged, she met a few more. Eventually, she met a man who took. They now live together, and the relationship looks durable.

What made the difference? The Internet slowed her down. She had a chance to get to know someone first through a correspondence by e-mail. She also was able to test the honesty of her Internet correspondent by meeting him later. Did his Internet persona match his actual living one? Not surprisingly, she met several men who were fascinating while hiding behind a computer screen, but who in person quickly revealed themselves to be terribly self-centered or insecure.

■ ■ ■ ■ ■

Do Any of These "Ifs" Apply to You?

If you dump all your troubles on people when you first meet...

When you first meet someone, do you have an irresistible tendency to tell him or her all your troubles? This is a very negative first step, especially if you think that you are only telling the truth. Even truth, if ill-timed, can be used as a hostile gesture. Dumping everything on people is similar to avoiding real issues—both are a reflection of your own insecurity. Initial encounters involve making a good impression. Don't exaggerate or overpraise yourself. Try to create a balanced atmosphere that permits truth telling, but wait until your relationship develops and the timing is right before revealing too much. Those feelings of inferiority or insecurity could dissipate in the context of an energizing relationship.

If you have been dumped on...

To the poor recipients of the dumping: Gently suggest to your partner that you are much more interested in hearing about the positive features of his or her life. Hearing about desirable characteristics is sexier. It's a nice way to say that whiners, complainers, or totally insecure people are not attractive. Attractive people value you enough to wait until trust develops before opening up some—but not all—of their emotional baggage on you.

If you repeatedly fall for unavailable partners...

This attachment-avoidance syndrome goes like this: You are looking for a heterosexual partner, but seem to be drawn to the clergy, married people, homosexuals, men or women who live in another city. Whatever the unconscious motivation, you can be reasonably sure of unhappy endings. Married people, even those on the verge of divorce (as they often claim), very seldom go on to the person with whom they are having an affair. It's a chaotic time for them, an emotional roller coaster with many mixed feelings—high highs and desperate lows. Divorced people seldom marry the "transition person." When they have healed and re-established their own lives, when they have found some peace and understanding about their marriage, only then will a healthy, long-term partnership be possible.

But if you have been the transition person and if you continually go for the unavailable relationship, then you need to ask yourself, "Why do I set myself up for failure?" Once in a while such a relationship works, but more often it reflects a person's low self-esteem, as well as a deep sense of unworthiness and lack of trust. In some cases, the man or woman may be playing a game of challenge and seduce, but the fun is over once the seduction is complete. So even if you win, you lose. You will be alone again, feeling safe that you have kept commitment away and stayed in control.

Some affairs, especially those in which one person is single or when both partners are married, can last for decades. There are such relationships that can be stable enough for all concerned. Except perhaps for the person in the couple who doesn't know or finds out very late—or too late. The breaking of a trust, whether successfully hidden or not, is always complicated and messy for all those concerned.

> *If you are playing with relationships on the Internet or on blind dates, arranged meetings, commercial dating services, or newspaper, television, and magazine matchmaking bulletin boards . . .*

Be aware that many people looking for partners don't tell the truth about themselves. Be careful when you're using any of these methods of developing a relationship. While there are some success stories, there are also grim accounts of con artists looking to exploit people. Arrange your meetings in public places. Never take a large amount of cash with you. Take a friend along with you and get a common-sense objective view. Are you convinced by the integrity of your Internet or bulletin board find? Check yourself. Are you emotionally vulnerable? Are you socially unsure of yourself? Has your computer dating through the Internet become a compulsion?

> *If you have sex after the first, or first few, dates...*

Don't do it. It invariably ends the relationship quickly. Despite progress toward equality, men still have sex because of the possibility of sex, and women have sex because it offers the possibility of love. "Promiscuity," as Tennessee Williams once wisely observed, may "represent the possibility of love" for both men and women, but it's a fruitless search. Give a new relationship time, then sex will mean more. Too many people jump into bed with each other's dissatisfactions in life, hoping they will somehow be made better. They never are, and the sex is almost always forgettable. In any case, never have sex with a stranger—a person you have only known for a month or two—without condoms. The risks are too great. A man who refuses to wear a condom saves you a lot of time—dump him immediately! He is not a caring person and is not to be trusted.

If you go to bars for pickups...

Go to Starbucks instead. Try the old grocery store checkout line pickup routine first. If you only hang out in bars looking for a date, you limit yourself only to those people who can't think of anything else to do either.

If TV is your main companion...

The world of television is a narrow world. It makes you passive and stupid. Even too much good TV (Public Television, for example) can be bad, simply because it is undemanding. It doesn't challenge you in any way. It does it all for you. Without real exercise, the mind, like the muscles, atrophy, grow smaller and weaker. The other factor that exists with programs like *The Jerry Springer Show*, *Survivor*, *Who Wants to be a Millionaire?*, and *Big Brother* is what might be called the "What's Missing from Your Life Factor?" Ask yourself, "What am I getting out of these shows?" Instead, check out my recommended reading list at the end of the book for a stimulating read. Interact with people. Take a language or dance class. Go to an art gallery. Start developing your capacity to find wonder in small frames that don't come with commercials. Listen to live jazz. One thing is certain: the most *boring* people in the world only talk about what they saw on TV.

Recovery after Divorce

There has been an enormous rise in divorce among people married for 15 years or more. Why? Perhaps it's due largely to a shift in attitude on the part of one of the partners. Or, expectations have changed for one or both partners. No doubt many of these couples from a more tradition-bound generation felt the healthy influence of the women's movement, which made it possible for relationships to be more egalitarian. In any event, these couples, like those of any generation, started out by being very much in love. They seemed, as the saying goes, "right for each other."

■ ■ ■ ■ ■

Claire, for instance, was enormously satisfied with a conventional marriage to Steve. Steve supported her and the two children. Claire worked part-time outside the home, but was responsible for all the cooking and household tasks as well as the childcare. They enjoyed a mutually satisfying sexual relationship. About 15 years into the marriage, they were no longer getting along. They had frequent arguments about sharing household tasks and childcare. She no longer felt close enough and loving enough to want to have sex. He felt deprived and angry, accusing her of a lack of sexual desire for neurotic reasons. Her desire, however, was as strong and healthy as ever. She was simply not willing to accommodate Steve, whom she no longer loved. Claire became increasingly more interested in an egalitarian relationship, resenting the submissive role Steve insisted on. When the two children went off to college, she made up her mind to divorce.

Steve felt his masculinity was threatened and saw no need to change. Yet people can and do change. Here's an example of a dramatic change that occurred in what was a very traditional marriage.

■ ■ ■ ■ ■

Diane married James at age 18. He was seven years older, had a college degree, and was a junior officer in the regular Army. After a passionate love affair, and the birth of their two children, it seemed as if they were settled into their traditional military life, which meant moving from base to base. When the children were in school, Diane became bored with the conventional expectations of an Army wife. In the meantime, James was preoccupied with his military rank and status. He quickly reached the goal of Lt. Colonel. He followed the routine of military life unquestioningly, seeing himself as a great patriot who participated in and supported the war in Vietnam. Diane, however, had many reservations, not only political ones. She began to feel the need for higher education. This generated many arguments between them. James didn't see a need for her to go to college. When she enrolled, the pressure at home was so intense it was obvious that they could no longer live together.

In the ensuing years, they both remarried. Neither marriage turned out well. James married a woman who quite happily accommodated all his wishes. Very soon, he was bored and began to miss the intellectual stimulation of Diane. He slowly realized that Diane had qualities he admired that he could not originally appreciate. She was bright, lively, engaging, and witty.

In the meantime, the children—now married adults—made it known they did not like their parents' new partners. They maintained good relations with both of them, and Diane and James started to meet more frequently at family events related to their children. Both noticed profound changes in each other. For one thing, James had second thoughts about U.S. involvement in Vietnam. For another, he respected Diane's new career as a social worker. Without making a commitment to remarry, they both divorced their current spouses. Within two years, Diane and James were single again.

This time, they decided to live together for an experimental period. Diane noticed her ex-husband's transformation into a more flexible and responsive person. James no longer felt threatened by her independence. His Army attitudes and behavior had mellowed. Both were no longer confined by the demands of a rigid Army hierarchy and etiquette. The simple fact is that they both matured and learned to respect each other. They both found that having separate interests did not interfere with a harmonious relationship.

Encouraged by their children and the good experience of living together, they decided to remarry. Over the years, it has turned out to be an incredibly successful marriage. Such a positive outcome after such an acrimonious divorce could not have been predicted.

■ ■ ■ ■ ■

It Pays to Make a Good Choice of Partner

Divorce law is not about justice or fairness or protecting anyone's rights or what's best for the child; it is big business.
— *NEW YORK* MAGAZINE,
DECEMBER 13, 1999

There are no failsafe methods to determine in advance whether a person you're in love with is right for you. We often see people who appear to be "the perfect couple." These same couples just as often get divorced. But it's not just a case of making a poor marriage and then undoing it. Today the stakes are higher. Even though some divorces still provide mutually satisfying settlements, there are an increasing number of horrendous and messy breakups that involve false accusations of child and spousal abuse to secure custody or to ensure larger alimony payments. When children are caught up in such divorces, the results can be disastrous.

Anybody who has been through a divorce knows exactly what I'm talking about. Even when a split was appropriate and necessary, people still say that the process itself was one of the most traumatic they had ever experienced.

So it's more crucial than ever to increase your chances of selecting the right partner.

· 8 ·

Before You Commit

Checking Out His/Her Family

Sometimes we are so swept away by our needs of the moment or by our lifelong and culturally conditioned notions of "romance" and "passion" that we become vulnerable to making unwise relationship choices. That's why it's crucial that we use some caution and common sense before making a serious life commitment with a partner.

Since one of the major themes of this book is that a majority of people choose the wrong partner, it pays to have as much knowledge as possible before another mistake is made. Of course, there are no guarantees. Some people have been lucky in love. They have impulsively married a partner within a short time, and the relationship has thrived.

These are the exceptions, however. Too many relationships do not get past the two-year mark, enough time for partners to realize that they do not share enough in life to go on together.

There are other pressures that may be hidden from you in the first flush of a new romance. In one case, a woman came to me suspecting that something was wrong because her partner would not introduce her to his family. Why is this important? Experience has shown me that it is of value for you to learn about the family context of your potential partner. What is your partner's attitude to her or his family? Does he have any family obligations that may weigh heavily on you later on?

In the above case, the woman eventually learned some critical information. Her potential partner, for instance, continued to be dominated by an abusive father, because that father was also his boss at work. The father held his son's purse strings. It was clear that marrying this man would also mean "marrying" the father. Did she want to do that? At least she had the information to make an informed decision.

I have also seen cases where heavy family debts that were hidden from a partner before marriage later added great stress on the relationship. Isn't it important for you to know that half your partner's salary may be going to his or her alcoholic brother, bedridden mother, or ex-spouse?

You might also take a look at your partner's friends, at the family history, and at his or her current relationship with Mom and Dad and any siblings. To what extent does her or his family accept you? Will that be important to you later on? Not that any of these things have to be relationship deal breakers, but it's good to know before making a serious commitment.

Getting Beyond the Wedding

When couples don't communicate about important issues, their relationship is likely to run into serious trouble.

■ ■ ■ ■ ■

One deeply divided couple, Robert and Karen, came to me after a short time as husband and wife. They recalled having been very much in love when they met. They enjoyed every spare moment together. After a wonderful trip to Italy, everything looked so good. They set a wedding date. In discussing their past together, they both particularly focused on the feverish excitement and diverting busyness of their wedding. So much had to be done! Who had time to think about issues like money, family, or where to live?

In looking back on all the joyful wedding preparations, they realized they had never had one serious discussion about their future. Even before the wedding, it became clear that Robert did not like her folks, and they didn't care for him. Both Robert and Karen remembered having private doubts, but said to themselves, "Why bother with that now, there will be plenty of time later."

The problem was that "later" always arrives sooner than we think. They recalled lots of discussions about such things as Karen's wedding dress, where to hold the wedding, and who not to invite. But they never discussed money, children, or even why Robert divorced his first wife.

The prognosis is not good for Robert and Karen, who impulsively focused on the fleeting joy of a gift-wrapped wedding, instead of on serious communication—the true gift—that every successful relationship needs.

■   ■   ■   ■   ■

Money Matters

Money is a loaded subject. It comes attached to many complicated feelings and issues, from both our childhood and adult experiences. Try to put all the money issues on the table: bank accounts (will they be separate, joint, or both?), insurance (especially health), and investments. Don't be afraid to ask, What happens if there is a breakup? Talk about it all: savings, joint purchases, individual responsibilities versus shared expenses. Talk about everything that could become difficult if there is no clear agreement.

Be clear about how you feel about money, and consider that compromises might have to be made with a partner who comes with his or her own notions about how the money "should" be handled.

Should you sign a prenuptial agreement? This is often a consideration that demands special knowledge. It's not my area of expertise, but here's one case where it became an issue.

■ ■ ■ ■ ■

Money became a divisive issue in Steven and Irene's case. This was an interesting example of a partner who equated money with love, which is not uncommon. Steven, the product of an arrogant father who emotionally abused him, made Irene sign a prenuptial agreement. They kept separate bank accounts. He obsessed over every dime they spent. When Irene wanted new furniture for the house they'd been living in for three years, it became a major crisis in the family, which now included two sons.

Ultimately, Irene had to divorce Steven. After one argument, he became so tightly strung and controlling that he pushed her down a flight of stairs. After about two years, Steven started making overtures that he'd been seeing a therapist and wanted to come back. He wanted to give marriage another chance. He wanted another child with Irene.

In the two-year period, Irene had found her own voice. She got help with the children and went back to work part-time. She wisely invested her $60,000 divorce settlement money, which Steven had tried to cheat her out of. (Irene, who had been working before she met Steven, knew enough to insist on a personal settlement that reflected the money she would have put away for her future. Instead, she had spent many crucial working years attending to Steven's needs and demands.) Irene also became passionate about her growing young sons and she took up tennis.

Irene did agree to remarry Steven, but this time she was stronger. She stood up to his controlling

tendencies *at the outset*, heading off future problems by refusing to sign a prenuptial agreement
this time around. Her extremely valuable insight,
which may have saved her marriage, was this:
"Steven equated money with love and control and
power. When he had the money, he did not have to
make a full commitment to me. He could always
get off the hook and take his money—his love and
power—with him. Without the prenuptial, Steven
pays more attention to our relationship, to *my*
needs, as well as his and our children's needs."

The couple did indeed have a third child, and
have been together for nine years since their
divorce. Sometimes it takes a major crisis to open
up the lines of communication, and for one or both
partners to find her or his own voice.

■ ■ ■ ■ ■

More about Communicating with Your Partner

I recently tested a couple about each partner's
likes and dislikes, values and interests. Each had
to predict what the other would say. "Oh, I know
exactly how Bert feels about that," Joy told me.
And Bert said, "Joy likes exactly what I like, feels

the same way I do about children and money." Well, can you guess what happened? Neither of them offered any right answers. They could not even guess their partner's favorite color and movies. The answers for Bert reflected *Bert's* favorite color and movies, and vice-versa for Joy.

This is why I recommend that couples try to have serious discussions about what turns them on and off within the first few months of their relationship. It's important to handle such serious talks with honesty *and* kindness. For example, try *not* to communicate with each other using these expressions:

- You don't love me.
- You don't listen.
- What's the matter with you?
- You hate me.
- Where are your brains?
- How many times do I have to tell you?
- Why did you?
- How could you?
- Why don't you?
- What's wrong with you?
- You always…
- You never…
- I don't want to talk about it.

Instead, try to say how you *feel* about whatever upsets you.

Try:

- I'm upset when…
- I'm sad when…
- I'm unhappy and worried when we can't talk nicely to each other.

Remember: Those "I messages" really can disarm and engage a defensive person.

What Do I Ask of a Divorced Partner with Children?

Since this book is about trying again after a failed love relationship, naturally many people will be coming out of potentially complicated divorces. If either partner has been divorced, try to discuss these issues:

- What went wrong with your previous partners.
- What exactly was the divorce settlement?
- If any children are expected to live with you, do you agree about child-rearing practices? (This could turn into a major source of conflict later on.)

- Are either of you similar to the person who preceded you?
- Which religion will the children be raised in? Would you agree to let *them* decide when they're of age?
- Your interests. Different interests don't have to be a problem, especially if you discuss them before a commitment.
- Your value system. Values are different from interests, because different values can cause great conflict. Issues like truthfulness, trust, ethics, cheating or stealing, health (drug use), and infidelity, matter. They cannot be ignored.

It's worth considering these issues. Poor communication or no communication at all inevitably creates bad situations. These situations invariably get worse after marriage.

Promises

Occasionally, I find myself counseling people who are forced to deal with a partner's promises to change. I tell them to try not to fall for promises like, "Don't worry, after we're married I'll stop doing drugs." Or, "Don't worry, I won't be unfaithful after we're married, but now I just need my freedom." Rarely are such promises kept.

Consider Not Making a Commitment

If any of the following apply to you, you might just consider not making a commitment at this time:

- You can't be available to each other for one full day without spending most of it watching TV.
- You can't figure out what to do about family members who present a problem to your relationship.
- You constantly argue about money. Money issues are very volatile, because they determine so much about our lifestyle.
- You don't, or did not in the past, have a good relationship with either parent and your partner behaves just like one of them. Or, if your partner is mean and nasty to his or her own parents.
- You suspect that your mate suffers from severe neurotic or character disorders, psychopathic behavior, or sexual perversions. In such cases, premarital counseling is always advised.

Don't Commit or Marry

If the following apply, I'd strongly advise against any type of commitment:

- Your partner is abusive, mocks you, and doesn't respect your intelligence.
- Your partner wants you to give up your friends.
- Your prospective partner has traits that you hate, such as a violent temper or unclean habits, and you avoid raising the issues for fear of giving offense.
- You have a hostile-dependent relationship, where you can't stand being with—or being apart—from each other. This is exhausting. Remember Sam and Diane on the television show *Cheers*? Their hostile-dependency did not work out, nor does it in real life!
- Jealousy is already a big issue between you.
- Your partner has an all-consuming hatred or prejudice for members of other races or ethnic groups. (I also advise women not to marry homophobic men. They are usually so preoccupied with defending or proving their masculinity that they rarely make suitable mates. Homophobia is not simply disagreeing with, or not liking, the gay

lifestyle. A homophobic person is more likely filled with anger and hatred, much like some people who are violently opposed to women's rights. It becomes a constant preoccupation, which is also seen in people who hate those of another race. Homophobics can be consumed with hate. In the film *American Beauty*, the abusive and homophobic father played by Chris Cooper has repressed his own homosexual impulses, so he lashes out against anyone who consciously or unconsciously stimulates or arouses these impulses.)

- Your partner abuses drugs or alcohol, or is addicted to sex. Addicts always give priority to their addiction—even over family and children.

- Your prospective partner is a gay or lesbian person, *and you think that you can change them into heterosexuals with love*. It rarely works. Sure, life is unpredictable, but be aware of the slim chances.

- You are pressured into a marriage. People who submit to such pressure often find that they become resentful, even consumed with rage, in response to any obstacle that later arises.

Testing the Relationship Waters

Sometimes it is much more important to find out what your partner feels, rather than arguing your point because you are sure you're right. That's one way to open the lines of communication and head off unpleasant surprises later on.

Here are a few questions to discuss gently with a partner. Avoid offering ultimatums, make no threats, and never accept promises like, "Once we're married, I'll change."

- Should you live together first?
- Should you spend a two-week holiday together abroad, without access to your working world?
- Does it matter that you both have very special separate interests or routines, such as Monday Night Football, porno films, workout nights with friends, all-day tennis sessions on the weekends?

For others, it could matter that a partner won't stop smoking—or even try—no matter how the other person feels about it. These seemingly little things can grate on a relationship, wearing it down. So the last consideration could be the most useful:

• Should you consider premarital counseling?

Adjusting Your Expectations

Once again, remember that unrealistic expectations in love often sabotage relationships before they have time to grow. So does a lack of communication between partners. It's always frustrating for me to hear people describe a potentially good relationship in their lives that was ended before it was allowed a chance to thrive.

■ ■ ■ ■ ■

Marthe, a 65-year-old widow, appeared to have found her second "dream man." He shared her cultural interests. He was handsome and wealthy, and he was crazy about her. She initiated counseling because, after a few sexual experiences, she was no longer sure he was right for her. "He doesn't turn me on," she complained. As revealed in counseling, Marthe had created an unrealistic expectation. She was comparing her new relationship to feelings she had when she was 20. The 20-year-old in her was very much in love with the man who became her husband. Could her youthful experiences be recaptured? That's a heavy burden for any new partner to bear. No, her new partner could not be her late husband. Stuck in the past, Marthe could not see this wonderful man for who he was. She could not adjust her expectations and give this man a chance to "turn her on."

Of course, Marthe's case wasn't really just about sex. It was about her grief, too—grief at getting old, at being alone, at having to start over when she still had many years left to live. Her attitude, quite hidden until she suddenly dumped him was, "How dare this new man—this interloper—think that our sex could compare to what I enjoyed with my late husband, the love of my life!"

The potential for complete satisfaction is always present, if the couple has the sensitivity to adjust to each other. Older people can certainly expect to have passionate sex. As Helen Gurley Brown boldly wrote in a *Newsweek* article on sex after 60, "I had sex last night. I'm 78 and my husband, movie producer David Brown, is 83. Shocking? Shouldn't be." Bravo, Ms. Brown! Understanding a bit about the physiology of aging, which can affect sexual response and performance, is useful in some cases. It's also important to remember that, at any age, a new relationship, while exciting, is also stressful.

Alas, Marthe didn't have the patience to see her relationship through. What could have developed into a perfectly acceptable or even marvelous relationship was prematurely terminated. Now 75, Marthe has become lonely and bitter, focusing on her regrets. The fallout from these negative feelings weighs heavily on her daughter. It is the daughter who must deal with Marthe's stubbornness about giving up the large house she no longer needs or can afford. It is the daughter who must hear, over and over, stories about how lonely she is. The mother's refusal to bury the past has made what should have been a joyous part of both their lives unnecessarily sad.

■ ■ ■ ■ ■

The Most Important Ingredients of a Successful Relationship

I never counted the number of lectures on love and marriage I've given all over the world. By now, that number would probably be somewhere in the thousands. Whenever I reveal the three absolutely most important ingredients of a successful partnership, audiences never fail to seem a bit shocked. Some audience members shout, "What about sex?" And, "Hey, Doc, what about attraction?" While these are important, they do not deserve to be in the top three. Why? Because if we're talking about a relationship with a real potential to grow and endure, sex and attraction too easily fall by the wayside over time.

The top three ingredients for a lasting partnership are:

1. A sense of humor.
2. The wisdom to overlook a lot of stuff.
3. A basic respect for each other, no matter what.

Ask yourself, without these three things, would it matter how attractive someone is? How good would sex be with a humorless sourpuss who obsesses over every little thing you do? Who does not respect you?

Additional Concerns

Here are some facts that might be worth pondering. Current data about Americans reveal that some 85 percent of all men and women eventually marry. (By contrast, in Scandinavia less than 50 percent of the population marries.) More than 60 percent of U.S. couples divorce or separate. Some 75 percent remarry, and almost 50 percent of these marriages fail. So it pays to be much more cautious the next time around.

I have detailed many reasons why most Americans choose the wrong partner. One critical aspect of this failure has not been emphasized enough. When we marry or commit to living with someone, it's a package deal. That means we also marry his or her heritage, history, family, responsibilities, rituals, friends, habits, unresolved anger—what some people call "baggage" and others call "garbage." Such a package often involves many positive features, in addition to what you already find attractive about your partner.

The vital question is: Have you been with your partner long enough to witness, explore, and appreciate most of the issues involved in his or her current life?

Some things to consider: financial obligations, commitments to a previous spouse, parental receptivity to the marriage or partnership, and responsibility for aging parents. Needless to say, you may want to marry whether family and friends want you to or not. But it pays to be aware of how they feel about your decision.

Self-Defeating Approaches
Some not very good approaches to a new marriage include:

- Looking mainly for traits opposite from the previous partner—if that's your only criteria, it's a road to disaster.
- Believing the illusion that this time around, everything will work without conflicts. Conflict-free marriages practically do not exist.
- Idealizing your new love. This is a sure way to repeat past mistakes.

Take your time before making a commitment. Wait until at least the passion—the "madly in love" period—has subsided. Then you can make a rational decision about someone you still like.

Mutuality Versus Self-Enhancement: Will I Lose My Identity?

Some people who are not sure they want another relationship after a difficult breakup may experience a sense of dread. They may be apprehensive about giving up their identity.

In such cases, the question arises: Should your goal be self-actualization or mutuality? The answer would appear to be simple, but it's not. I've found that many people have made accommodations and compromises so that growth could occur within the context of their special relationship. Sometimes such a relationship is a rewarding one. In our culture, however, a great emphasis is placed on personal autonomy as the goal for people searching to live their lives more fully. In this book, I have returned to that idea time and again: We all need to find our own individuality before we can enjoy a full and lasting partnership with someone else.

That's true—up to a point. For example, people who act as if they are more important than you, who don't respect your individuality, or who don't display any loving concern for you, are clearly not worthy partners for anyone. Many breakups occur after a partner decides he or she will no longer allow himself or herself to be exploited by an insensitive and selfish person.

But do we need "to find ourselves" totally before we look to another person? It's a paradox, because without some reasonable self-sacrifice, compromise, and genuine give-and-take on our part, no successful relationship would be possible.

Autonomy is rewarding, yes, but autonomy within the context of a supportive and loving partnership is even better. A couple can thrive on a healthy mutuality, in which intimacy and sharing increases one's connection to a mate. A strong relationship values mutuality as highly as self-actualization.

In mutuality, there is no sense of self-sacrifice. Each partner supports the other. The feeling of self-worth that follows is life enhancing. Neither partner is diminished within the relationship. Individuals work toward their goals with a partner's support.

Like almost everything in life, mutuality is a process that demands sensitive and caring communication skills. These skills are learned. No one is born with them. The problem for women, as many have noted, is that they are often reluctant to speak up when they feel threatened or misunderstood. They are particularly hesitant when a relationship is in its early stages. But I urge all of you, women *and* men, to tell your partner what you are feeling. Get the potential issues of domination and control out in the open. Only then will the process of give-and-take slowly start to take root.

Recently, I was waiting in line at Carnegie Hall when I saw a woman in her 30s timidly ask her slightly older boyfriend, "Is it all right if I wait over here?" It was as if she was asking a parent permission, rather than saying, "Honey, I'll feel more comfortable if I wait over here." One can only guess what was going on between them, but such subtle lines of control and potential conflict are often hardwired into a person's family. They need to be revealed and discussed early in a relationship *before* they become a serious threat to your potential for sharing a healthy mutuality.

Two individuals can accomplish more together than either can alone. A loving partnership means two people *sharing* the voyage to finding each one's own voice.

Making Your Past Failures Work for You

Once you get over your own self-loathing, it feels pretty good to stick up for yourself. And there's no turning back.
—CAMRYN MANHEIM

Putting a troubled love history behind you is easier said than done. It is not unlike an adult trying to deal with a victimized childhood, a trauma that carries over into adulthood. It then becomes vitally important to learn to trust and love again. The same is true with failed relationships, especially when a betrayal is involved. Can you risk being hurt again? Will you allow yourself the time with another potential partner to create the circumstances that foster a caring and trustworthy relationship?

The first thing you can do is to accept this essential and absolute fact: You don't have to be crippled by the mistakes of the past. That's right. By consciously raising the question of what can be learned from the past, you can face and discuss what happened. It's always helpful to give a close friend permission to suspend worrying about your feelings. That way, you can have a real discussion. For someone who really wants to explore past failures, honesty is precious.

Many people ask, "Where did I go wrong?" And, "What mistakes did I make?" These are good questions, but dwelling on them can be destructive if it generates a type of passive self-pity. You need to use whatever knowledge you gain and move on.

Use it to fuel your determination to learn from that experience and not make the same mistakes.

What Am I Doing Wrong?

Here's a checklist. People who have had repeated failures in love relationships most typically make these mistakes over and over again:

- They bring unrealistic expectations to a new relationship.
- They fail to take the time to let a friendship develop first.
- They allow the sexual-passionate early stage of love to rule them.
- They fall for a partner's spontaneity and energy before determining if that partner can also be a responsible and caring person.
- They interpret jealousy and abuse to mean, "We love each other."
- They allow a breakup to make them feel unworthy, when in fact many breakups are entirely the responsibility of the partner.
- They often carry the burden of a breakup that was simply out of their control, where nobody was really at fault.

- It's probably a good idea to reflect on the possibility that it wasn't totally the partner's fault or responsibility. (All right, maybe *most* of it.) Take this opportunity to reflect on your role in the breakup.
- Consider the possibility, however sad or unhappy or guilty you may feel about the breakup, that it was not a workable relationship, and that there is someone out there who will offer you a happier and healthier partnership.

Dealing with Anger

After a breakup, there will be a certain level of anger directed at oneself or the partner. Unresolved anger can keep you feeling victimized. Often, such unresolved feelings can put you into a dysfunctional or destructive mode. In some cases, as an act of revenge, one partner destroys or steals the property of the former lover.

Often, people use a negative breakup experience to make self-defeating generalizations, such as "All men are jerks" and "All women care about is money." This is part of the destructive baggage that must be gotten rid of before you can freely move on.

This is not to say that you can avoid being angry or that forgiveness is the only way to go. But while it's important to acknowledge these emotions, many people don't realize that by not liberating yourself from the anger, your ex-partner still maintains power over you.

Here are two ways of moving from angry disillusionment to constructive hopefulness. One is philosophical; the other uses action to heal. Reflect deeply and honestly on these two approaches:

1. Who am I? What do I really want? The next time around, can I find my own voice?
2. Perform some acts of kindness. Even if it takes some effort, be kind and compassionate to your friends, neighbors, family—and, most of all, to yourself. Consider doing something very special, like taking a trip, throwing a party, shopping, or going out to dinner with your friends. If money is an issue, there are a lot of simple and enjoyable things to do, like meditating, yoga, hiking, immersing yourself in a relaxing bubblebath, or taking trips to a favorite museum.

These ideas may seem simplistic, and you may not even feel like doing them, but you'll be surprised. They relieve tension, alter your mood for the better, and they could be the first step in turning your life in the direction you want it to go.

Defusing Anger: Using "I Messages"

Closeness is achieved and maintained not only through the sharing of endearments and loving gestures. In intimate relationships, there also needs to be ample room for anger and arguments, bad moods, and short tempers. These emotions are among the most difficult for lovers to accept and understand in each other.

Naturally, when a bad mood continues for too long, therapy may be advisable. But, in most cases, bad moods pass. A partner's short temper can also be a barrier to communication. In such cases, using "I messages" can avoid or defuse an argument before it gets out of hand. For example, say, "I worry that I can't tell you how I really feel," rather than "You never listen to me."

The use of "I messages" enhances your level of understanding, as well as increasing the likelihood that you will be heard and understood. This form of communication can also help defuse some of the toxic anger that grows out of conflicts in which past hurts rise again. Indeed, dragging up old woes during an argument puts your partner on the defensive, and the potential for a fair and open disagreement goes out the window. Problem resolution comes most easily when both people understand the rules of fair engagement. Hitting a partner over the head with an offensive "You message" only creates a barrier to communication. The goal is to really listen to a partner, to understand feelings as well as words.

Phrases to avoid during an argument? "You never…" and "You always…" as in, "You never take me out," or, "You always make all the decisions." Along with name-calling, these offensive "You" messages should be avoided at all costs. For one thing, they incite another person to argue with you. For another, they escalate and intensify an argument destructively by pitting one partner against the other.

On the other hand, try saying, "I worry because we don't go out much." Or, "I feel upset because I want to be part of important family decisions." If you're angry, then say, "I'm upset because we can't seem to have a discussion without getting angry at each other." Or, "I feel frustrated because I don't feel cared for." Such an approach neutralizes to a great extent the attack-counterattack reflex, allowing for the possibility of a rational discussion of what really matters.

Here are a few more examples:

- "I feel troubled about what happened, but I want to hear your side of the story."
- "I'm upset, but I want to know how you feel."

Focus on what's bothering you. Then devise an "I message" that locates the emotion you are feeling. In this way, "I messages" can allow for a clear communication about a particular situation. It's a good way to make a productive discussion possible.

Don't expect this strategy to be effective immediately, but stick with it. It will eventually work. In fact, if it does not work, it's a good sign that this relationship may be wrong for you. Open and fair communication is a key dimension of a mature relationship.

If you want to be heard, use "I messages." If you want to understand what your partner is trying to say, put your ego away and listen well.

· **9** ·

Growing Into Love

It takes courage and faith to believe that our lives will become richer and more fulfilling by our efforts to grow in love. If you have made mistakes in past relationships, you are probably smarter for the experience, as well as hurt by it, regardless of who did what to whom. Correcting such errors in judgment can become the mechanism for making your next relationship work. This time around, you might select a person who is more likely to fulfill your needs. You might change yourself in some significant way, or both.

Reconciling differences is a key element in allowing us to grow in love relationships. When partners feel pressured to change, they tend to become defensive, to withdraw, or to become aggressive. When partners feel accepted and understood, they are more likely to change willingly.

In any case, use your experience to your benefit. Meeting new people may initially feel like trying to mix oil and water. Be aware that with another person, however, it may be possible to develop a deep relationship that would have been impossible before. Both the new person and lessons learned from your old experience may potentially be working in your favor. There will be challenges, but working with a different partner may prove pleasantly surprising. Especially if you have found your own voice, a new relationship could provide the strength and encouragement you need to thrive.

Damage Control

On the other hand, some new relationships that occur shortly after a breakup are ill advised. All bets are off, for example, if you go after the same mean and abusive type of person as your previous partner. If this is the case, you have yet to understand something very important about yourself.

Ask yourself: Why am I afraid of finding my own voice? Am I afraid of being alone, even for a short time, to heal and grow? Is that one reason I keep stumbling back into partners who wish to crush my uniqueness?

Surviving Abusive Relationships: You Make the Choice

If you have suffered from abuse and mistreatment, no matter how severe, you need to believe that you are not damaged for life. Forgiving or forgetting are not the issues of greatest importance. More crucial is working to make sure that the *rest* of your life reflects the best of you—and not the worst of the person who hurt you.

Your responsibility is to become the best person you can. Move away from whatever ugliness you experienced toward the fullness of your own potential. It will take time, perhaps years, to heal. But years from now, you are still going to be you. Your freedom from past hurts lies in the fact that the choice is yours. It's exactly the same for everyone. We start becoming loveable as soon as we recognize that it is something we want to do for ourselves. Retaining feelings of hatred and anger are often expressions of powerlessness. This is your time to be strong for yourself and others.

Can You See the Elephant in Your Living Room?

There's an old saying that if there's an elephant in your living room, you know it. The challenge is finding the most effective method of removing it from the premises! Your "elephant" may be certain personality traits that are sabotaging your efforts to go for the relationship you want. Perhaps there are certain behaviors or prejudices you might want to discard. No doubt you already have an idea of what prevents you from finding love, comfort, and peace in a relationship with others. So jump-start your efforts in removing that "elephant" from your living room by making a personal list of counterproductive personality and character traits. That's one way to begin gaining control over those seemingly unwieldy and surely unwanted behaviors.

A Sample List to Take into Your Next Relationship

Here's one list I've found to be effective over the years. I've spoken about people who court failure in relationships by bringing high expectations with them—by holding onto false notions of romance or demeaning idealizations of a partner. Those inevitably set us up for disappointment. On the other hand, what if you discovered in yourself, and in a potential partner, the following 10 qualities? You might use them as shared goals for your next relationship.

1. *Intimacy*—This is the closeness and trust that comes from making the effort to communicate

with a partner. It's one major indicator of our ability to sustain a caring, loving relationship through good times and bad.

2. *A sense of humor*—If you're willing to laugh at yourself and the world at large, you're probably someone worth knowing and a pleasure to hang out with. This trait is so attractive that it often makes up for what is lacking in other areas. And laughter is a compulsory skill when it comes to bringing up children.

3. *Honest communication*—Being open and good listening skills are something we develop with practice. It is important to avoid saying "I don't want to talk about it" when dealing with conflicts.

4. *Shared values*—Partners can have different interests. In fact, different interests make for a stronger relationship. On the other hand, do not expect a relationship to grow or last if you and your partner differ about values. If one partner wants children, and the other does not, for example, that's a certain deal breaker. It also helps if partners share ethical and/or spiritual goals. A feeling of common destiny, and a strong sense of loyalty, should pervade the relationship.

5. *Equality*—The success of a relationship increases enormously when partners have a conscious sense of the importance of respect for each other as individuals, and when they are willing to share responsibility in career, leisure, child rearing, and lifestyle choices. A commitment to each other's growth in career, talents, and sense of purpose or cause is very important.

6. *A sense of adventure*—A desire to keep the relationship fresh by finding new and interesting ways of expressing affection for each other.

7. *Shared experience*—A relationship grows over time, filled with a repository of mutual undertakings, private conversations, quiet intimacies, and shared thoughts on issues, as well as on celebrations, rituals, and traditions you both share.

8. *Respect for each other's feelings and wishes*—The willingness to delay one's own short-term desires in the knowledge that a similar willingness will exist on the part of the other person at a later time. Respect for each other's choice of friends and different leisure time interests. Specifically, respect for a partner's feelings toward sex in any given instance.

9. *Passion*—This does not mean just a healthy, robust sex life. Many people in lasting relationships have spoken to me about how they delight in their partner's "passion" for tennis, or "passion" for art. You may not share that passion, but that's what makes it so thrilling to see in a partner.

10. *Sharing in domestic duties*—A partner who accepts responsibility for doing a fair share of the more unpleasant household or family tasks is very attractive indeed. It's important not to be limited by gender stereotypes. It's not a good idea to allow a situation where one partner can take on a martyr role, claiming a monopoly on all the household tasks. This also carries over to having a responsible attitude about money.

I have said that these attitudes and behaviors can be learned. Some may say that people don't change, they *intensify* as they get older, because they are too set in their ways. But I have seen them change and grow out of the worst kinds of traits and prejudices into more understanding and open human beings. In this, as in most matters regarding relationships, communication is the key.

To conclude this section, I refer you to the valuable insight of a brilliant British novelist:

We are not the same person this year as last; nor are those we love. It is a happy chance if we, changing, continue to love a changed person.

—W. SOMERSET MAUGHAM

Is Conflict Good for Your Relationship?

A lot of people seem to want to make the institution of marriage substitute for a real relationship.

—SUSAN FALUDI

Perfect compatibility is a fantasy. Remember that scene from the film *Annie Hall* when Alvy (played by Woody Allen) goes up to a happy-looking young couple and asks them their secret? The woman answers, "I'm very shallow and empty and I have no ideas and nothing interesting to say." Her man says, "And I'm exactly the same way." Well, there you have one idea of what a conflict-free relationship might be like!

Conflict is a natural development between two people. Long-term relationships, ones that survive beyond the seemingly conflict-free, sexual-passionate stage, invariably involve arguments, tensions, upsets, and misunderstandings. Getting conflict out on the table is a good idea, because it paves the way for some kind of resolution or acceptance between partners.

While it's true that if nothing is confronted, nothing can be resolved, keep in mind that not every issue is subject to conflict resolution. Often, issues arise that require respect for differences and compromises by one—or both—partners.

How does your new partner handle conflict? Ever hear the expression, "When the sea was calm, all ships alike showed mastership in floating"? Well, so goes a relationship. How does your partner handle the sea when it's storm-tossed, or when there's a small leak in the boat? That will tell you a lot. In terms of conflict resolution, is your new partner the same as your old one? Some people rebound too fast. In desperation, they marry or commit again to the same kind of person that made for an unsuccessful relationship. Perhaps the new partner is financially unstable, or too controlling— just like the old partner. You won't see the real issues in the initial passionate-irrational stage of a relationship; they will reveal themselves in the conflicts that will inevitably occur.

Almost As Many Second Marriages Break Up As the First

This is why love the second time around is more demanding. Yes, you should know better. A second marriage or partnership asks for more patience, hesitation, and sensitivity. But don't be too hard on yourself if you suddenly discover you have fallen for the same type of person that is wrong for you. However, DO try to avoid continuing this relationship, so that you may be open to a more healthy and lasting one.

■ ■ ■ ■ ■

Beth is one person who caught herself in time. Sure, Ron was handsome and made an acceptable living, but he was also selfish and uncaring, just like her first husband. When she decided enough was enough, she told Ron the relationship wasn't working. "The real monster I suspected might be lurking within him really came out," she recalls.

"He screamed and yelled, and called me all kinds of horrible names. There was no discussion. That's when I knew it really was over. It hurt at first. What a fool I'd been. All the signs were there—the lack of caring and respect for my wishes and needs. Now that some time has passed, what a relief that he's gone!"

Beth gained more self-respect by ending the relationship to Ron. She is stronger now, knows more about what she's looking for in a relationship, and is more unwilling than ever to settle for another Mr. Wrong. She wants a full partner in life, one who respects her as a full partner too.

Not everyone is condemned to repeat past mistakes. Beth realized that her chances of meeting a caring person who respects her, and who therefore can potentially move into a mature love relationship, has increased. She has never been more optimistic, but she is wary too. That's good!

■ ■ ■ ■ ■

Effects on the Children

Be especially patient and sensitive when a potential partner has children. Don't move in as a mother- or father-figure immediately. Meet the child or children in a friendly social, non-disciplinary manner—*not* initially as a potential authority figure or parent.

What effect is your breakup having on your own children? Inevitably, there may be feelings of rational and irrational guilt. Either way, you can overcome the "woe-is-me" stage by making it an active concern. That is, you can start to take command by using your new situation in a productive way. Ask yourself, Can I make this relationship work? How can I avoid the same harmful effect that another breakup would bring?

The Death of a Partner: The "Rebecca" Syndrome

We all know the story of *Rebecca*, about a woman who marries a British nobleman, but feels tortured by living in the shadow of his first wife. As that story shows, making comparisons quickly wears a relationship out. Men and women both do it. Making comparisons is the greatest risk to any new relationship. It's hard not to do it, but if you want your new relationship to have a ghost of a chance, stop making comparisons to other people.

Warning Signs

- *Lack of Respect*— If you've just broken up or gotten divorced, you should be especially sensitive to a partner who does not give you the respect you deserve. Be on the lookout for any signs of a lack of caring about your integrity as a person. Everyone deserves respect at all times.

- *The Need for Independence*—Does your partner show a lack of awareness of your need to have an independent life? If so, that's not good. If you allow this, you may have no life of your own, or you will have a greatly reduced chance of living a full one. In some cases, a person ends up duplicating the former failed relationship by accommodating the other person's wishes, orders, or whims.

The irony of it all was, now that I had found something that made me feel good about myself, I had become interesting to other people and I started to get acting work. A little work as an interpreter, a little work as an actor. Things were looking up.

—CAMRYN MANHEIM

· 10 ·

Sex, Intimacy, and Friendship

The more things change, the more they remain the same. Here are a few thoughts that I've had over the years as a therapist and speaker that still remain relevant today:

Many aspects of the alleged sexual revolution appear actually to be part of an anti-sexual revolution. Among its main characteristics are the following:

- People have sex shortly after meeting, and then consider getting to know each other. But the possibility of a relationship is often sabotaged by the morning after. It's as if the old fairy tale of the frog and the princess has been rewritten with a contemporary twist: Today the princess kisses the prince, and he turns into a frog and hops away.

- People use sex as a test or a proof of love by saying in effect, "If you really love me, you'll have sex with me," or, "Since our sex together isn't so great, we must not love each other."

- There is a widespread failure to understand that individuals get hurt because they don't feel loved, not because they don't know how to make love.

Within the anti-sexual revolution, people see sex as an avoidance of, rather than an expression of, caring and intimacy. Sam Keen, a well-known psychologist and author, has commented, "When our Eros is limited to genital sexuality it becomes obsessive, and boring, and finally destructive." The negative side of our heralded sexual revolution offers little comfort to millions of lonely, alienated people needing love but getting laid instead.

The point is that although sex and attraction are important, love cannot take root or flower without intimacy.

The Rules of Attraction (There Are No Rules)

There is no particular physical appearance that is attractive to all people. The rules of attraction are an odd game at best. I know a woman who found a man's voice so attractive that his other attributes didn't matter. Of course, as her relationship developed, character issues became more important. But initially it was the man's voice that made her feel he was right for her. No matter what you look like, or how you perceive yourself, there's no accounting for the mystery of attraction.

Before you spend a lot of time and money trying to fit a particular model of femininity or masculinity, keep in mind that the element of initial attractiveness wanes very quickly. With just one brief conversation, the matter of attractiveness regarding a particular person can disappear. You may keep an ideal of attractiveness forever in your mind. Our advertising and television culture almost insists on it. Once you come to know a person, however, it's unlikely that your acceptance or rejection will be based on such a shallow ideal as attractiveness alone.

The Attraction Trap

As a practicing therapist, I've heard ex-lovers say things like, "I can't stand the sight of him." Or, "I could kill her." Why do supposedly great, passionate love affairs turn so easily to hate when the breakup comes? One reason may be that because the initial attraction promises so much, the letdown produces a more intense and irrational sense of betrayal.

No relationship can sustain the weight of unrealistic expectations thrust upon it. For that reason, many relationships are doomed from the start. Take a relationship between two moody, high-strung, and demanding people like writer Philip Roth and actress Claire Bloom. Here's how they described their initial attraction:

> *I recognized his tense, intellectually alert face immediately from photographs. Tanned, tall, and lean, he was unusually handsome; he also seemed to be well aware of his startling effect on women. I was immediately attracted to him…*
>
> —CLAIRE BLOOM,
> *LEAVING A DOLL'S HOUSE*

He shows up at some party, and there she is. There is this lonely actress in her 40s, three times divorced, and there's this new face, this new guy, this tree, and she's needy, and she's famous, and she surrenders to him…

—PHILIP ROTH,
I MARRIED A COMMUNIST

Each book was written after they divorced. One can hear in Bloom's almost nostalgic voice the disappointment of their failed relationship. Roth's voice is harsher and more defensive. He seems to be saying, "She was too needy. That's why the marriage failed. It wasn't my fault."

Often, there's a sense of personal failure, the feeling that one is somehow responsible for the end of a relationship. In such cases, ex-partners may find the responsibility is too much to bear. Our fragile egos set up a protective net of blame, and that manifests itself in angry statements such as, "It's all Miss Birdbrain's fault," or, "Mr. Fathead would just sit around and watch TV all day."

It is especially sad when children are caught in this net. They become a captive audience to the immaturity of two adults. They are forced to bear a largely hidden emotional burden that arises from the terrible, and totally unnecessary, spectacle of parents who, once in love, now hate each other.

One predictor of a successful relationship the second or third time around is an adult who takes responsibility for his or her actions. I have seen potentially destructive divorces handled well, where "damage control" protected the children, anger was managed, and the former spouses recovered faster and later each had a healthier, more lasting relationship with a new partner.

Looking Beyond the Physical

Let's face it. Men often make judgments about a woman based on physical appearance. Women, too, can be just as superficial. More than one woman has come to me and said, "Oh, there's Joe. He's wonderful and pleasant and so nice to me, but he doesn't turn me on. But there's Jim, who is handsome, an alcoholic, a gambler, a liar, but, wow, he really turns me on." Too many people marry the person who "turns them on." Sadly, most of these relationships fail within a year.

Getting Beyond Media Rules of Attraction

Advertising and Hollywood movie images often convey the message that only very attractive people marry each other. As a psychotherapist, I'll let you in on one of the secrets of the trade: the vast majority of these marriages don't last.

As someone once said about the idealized romantic films that permeate our culture, "Think about what happens to the couple when the film ends." One classic film, *Marty*, is a rare exception. The story deals with two seemingly unattractive but just-right-for-each-other people who fall in love. Peer pressure nearly destroys the relationship (Marty's friends describe his girl as a "dog"). They insist, partly out of jealousy, that she's not right for him. Fortunately, love is—believably, realistically—triumphant.

The film, which won Ernest Borgnine an Oscar, is still a refreshing romantic story that goes beyond the typically reductive Hollywood and advertising industry mentality. The couple in *Marty* respect each other, are helpful and communicative about trying to realize their dreams together, and don't run whenever there's a problem. They try to solve them. That's one reliable predictor of a relationship's future success. The woman in *Marty* (played by Betsy Blair), for instance, suggests ways that Marty can open his own business, instead of continuing to deal with a load of anxiety as an employee.

Even though this 1955 motion picture reflects a time of changing traditional male and female roles, Marty himself seems like a guy ready to respect his wife's needs, whether they might include going back to school, or perhaps getting or changing a job. By showing that romance and friendship are not only compatible, but desirable, *Marty* still speaks eloquently to us today.

The Sex Test

If you have poor sex with a new partner, does it usually end your relationship before it even begins? People complain about this a lot. They are confused when their first sexual experience with a new partner does not work out. This may seem obvious to some, but it's a very special point to understand. The early, and especially the first, sexual intercourse experience, is hardly ever an indication of how a love affair will turn out. It doesn't matter whether the initial experience is fantastic, disappointing, or a disaster.

Unfortunately, a failed or less-than-exhilarating first sexual experience often terminates a new relationship before it has a chance to begin. Whether it's performance anxiety, too much alcohol, or a physical problem, it's helpful to know that sexual inadequacy, if handled with sensitivity, can be resolved. It's also important to understand that a man or woman with no sexual performance problems may not, in the long run, be as suitable for you as a partner who is initially nervous, clumsy, or dysfunctional.

The best approach in these situations is a calm, nonjudgmental attitude that focuses on communication, caressing, and enjoying physical intimacy without intercourse. Only in some cases is outside counseling needed to resolve a sexual problem.

The point is that you can't tell from early sexual encounters whether the prospects are good for a committed relationship. In fact, great or poor sex in the early dating stages will not give you a clue one way or another as to whether a person is right for you.

There's a reason why your chances for a relationship may be even better with someone who demonstrates insecurity or inadequate sexual performance early on. Such so-called "inadequacy" may actually reflect an especially sensitive person who needs the patience and respect of a partner before feeling secure with sex. Often, the sexy "macho man" turns out to have an insensitive, uncaring side and makes a poor marital partner.

If you are worried about sexual adequacy or performance, and if it seems to be getting in the way of your relationships, then try talking about sex beforehand with a potential partner. People who desire sexual intimacy are likely to be understanding and sympathetic. Suggest cuddling, kissing, touching, massage, and even mutual masturbation. Take turns being passive or active, without sexual intercourse, until you feel comfortable or ready. Keep in mind that those who respond unsympathetically are not good for you anyway, so you haven't lost anything.

Touching, Cuddling, Caressing

Studies have shown that women generally agree that what they enjoyed the most about physical closeness was touching, cuddling, and caressing—more than sexual intercourse itself. About fifteen years ago, Ann Landers, the nationally syndicated columnist, asked her female readers which they preferred, and whether they would be willing to give up "the act" in order to be held close and treated tenderly. Of the more than 90,000 women who responded, 72 percent said yes, they would give up intercourse for cuddling. But it was also clear that they still liked intercourse, as long as cuddling was part of the lovemaking.

These findings illustrate how closeness and sensuality are indeed the main ingredients in a mutually intimate relationship. They also suggest that many men have been socialized to dissociate sex from intimacy.

Confused Messages about Love

Many people who have trouble sustaining relationships, or who are apprehensive about the possibility of sabotaging future relationships, worry about overcoming a past that may have included physical and emotional abuse. In one case, a 17-year-old male in a detention center told me this story. "My father beat the hell out of me while I was growing up. The more abusive he was, the more strongly he insisted that he was disciplining me because he loved me."

The young man asked me, "Do you think my father really loved me?" "No," I replied. "When someone brutalizes you, they're giving you a clear message. Maybe your father thought it was love, but that's not what love is."

Subsequent conversations revealed that the boy's father was also a victim of parental physical abuse.

"Then what should I do about it?" he asked.

"Take revenge," I said. "Living well is the best revenge. When you marry and have children of your own, don't beat them up, don't hit them . . . be gentle, caring, and respectful of them. That's the best chance you'll have of becoming a loving person, instead of a victim or a victimizer."

In another case, I was confronted on *Oprah* with an abused woman. She told of being repeatedly battered by her boyfriend. I asked why she stayed with him. "I love him, and he loves me," she said.

I replied: "Loves you? He doesn't even like you."

We need to help people distance themselves from the abusive behavior that spoils their capacity for mature relationships. And what about forgiveness? That's only possible and workable after a person has achieved an inner stability that frees him or her from identifying with the aggressor.

Being a Sensual Person

Being a sensual person, outside of the context of sexuality, is something we can do to improve our lives. Enjoy life's little pleasures on a regular basis. Pay attention to all the things you are doing. Get in the habit of living in the present. Enjoy your morning shower, instead of running the day's schedule through your mind. Prepare your meals as though you fully intend to enjoy eating them, and then focus on the different flavors of the food as you eat. Listening to music and eating by candlelight can be most pleasurable.

These are simple suggestions that cost little to do, but they can make every day full of small, gratifying moments. Learn new pleasures as well. If you only listen to one kind of music, expand your repertoire. Almost every kind of music offers something that gives pleasure and inspiration. You just have to listen to it, really listen. Make your commute to work an experience to enjoy. Try listening to books-on-tape to and from work.

Body Therapy

If you are not sure how to go beyond hugging and kissing in a new relationship, an uncomplicated massage might be just the thing. The useful book, *The Art of Sensual Massage*, will help make both partners sensitive to their entire bodies. Even better, go to a professional masseuse or masseur (not a sex worker) a few times and experience what it's like. Remember: It doesn't hurt to try something new. You'll probably like it.

This practice, also known as "body therapy," is especially useful for relatively healthy people who have problems with their body image. People with serious sexual problems frequently need therapeutic intervention as well.

In exploring these different dimensions of intimacy, I hope it's clear that the greatest sex is found in an intimate relationship.

What we all probably know in our hearts but fail to acknowledge is that there is no perfect person awaiting our arrival and that no orgasm has much significance outside of a relationship. Each person is flawed in some way but has the potential to be a wonderful friend and lover. Each sexual experience outside of a relationship is like a whiff of poppers or a toke of grass. They frequently provide momentary pleasure but they are only a distraction from the real need to love and be loved.

—BRIAN MCNAUGHT

Dating Pressures: Acting Out of Character

We all try to act and be at our best especially when dating someone new. But what happens when we act out of character, creating a "presentation self" that inaccurately reflects our real selves?

For example, have you ever tried to win a partner by impressing them with your flawless character? Are you an impatient person who can act as though you have the patience of Job? These are shams that become increasingly difficult to maintain. Many people explode under its weight, and that doesn't make a very good impression at all. More often, these people leave the relationship suddenly, placing the blame on the other person. This destructive cycle is called setting yourself up for failure.

This cycle can be broken. Consider the larger issue at work. Why try to misrepresent yourself in the first place? You will still have the fault, but now you will have added deception to it. It's better to acknowledge that your impatience is something you are working on. Ask the other person to help you become more tolerant in those situations that test your composure. The fact that you are aware of your fault gives the other person an opportunity to admire your honesty and commitment to learn new ways of overcoming this unattractive trait.

On Being Intimate with Yourself

When you don't have a partner, what do you do? For one thing, it's a great opportunity to work toward finding your own voice. Take care of yourself by working on achieving intimacy with people through friendship. Be patient. It is through friendship that the best and most lasting relationships develop and grow.

Many people who have come to me over the years have been overly concerned with their looks. They attribute the absence of a partner in their lives to their unattractiveness. Usually, I ask them to consider the people they know who are in relationships or married. Are they happy? If so, are they necessarily the best-looking people? In one case, a woman described her best friend as "short and heavy," but said she was "very happily married to a skinny unattractive guy." She soon realized my point. When two people love each other, sexual attraction and intimacy can emerge.

Still uncertain, she asked, "But how can I get someone to love me?" The first thing is not to get hung up on your looks. People who hate themselves and express it in *acting*—not actually looking— unattractive, tend to repel rather than attract others. Believing that certain perfumes, hair tonics, hygienic sprays, or selected sexual techniques will make you attractive gets you nowhere. A person who understands his or her self-worth and who is genuine becomes appealing to others.

In their book, *Men Like Women Who Like Themselves*, Steven Carter and Julia Sokol make encouraging statements about women, self-respect, and dating that also apply equally to men. For example, "The smartest woman knows that she always wants to be remembered for who she is, not how she looks or what she's wearing. She always checks in with herself before she checks herself out in the mirror and heads out the door."

I've learned an amazing truth from seeing so many people in therapy over the years. Many of the most attractive people see themselves as too thin, too fat, too ugly because of a facial mole (poor Cindy Crawford!), you name it. It's perhaps interesting to note that whether they are model-type pretty or handsome, or feeling unattractive, most people need to be reminded of what counts. Their sensitivity, sense of humor, intelligence, energy, character, interests—all these most attractive qualities need to be brought out. Here are examples of five conventionally "attractive" people I've seen in counseling. All of them can't seem to find and keep a partner:

1. *Jim, 29*: Charming and bright, Jim has an excellent income as a computer specialist. He makes friends easily among males and females. Women go crazy over him. He has a steady relationship for a month or two, then leaves her. Early on, he had a couple of bad sexual encounters. As a result, he's fearful of trying again—fearful of intimacy and falling in love. He decided to seek counseling to deal with why his relationships with women are superficial and non-sexual.

2. *Susan, 32*: A talented artist and business-woman who won't let any man get close to her. Therapy revealed that she's still coping with a rape that occurred 12 years ago.

3. *Bill, 29*: Quiet, sensitive, and sensual, Bill is always touching. As soon as he meets a woman he likes, he wants to sleep with her. He's attracted to intelligent, independent, and caring women. Bill's a social worker. But women uniformly resent him. Although he doesn't mean to be, Bill's too pushy. Some deep insecurity about women and intimacy has made Bill's life miserable.

4. *Seymour, 32*: He's a wonderful fellow, a university instructor who constantly falls for the wrong woman. If she has a different religion and value system, if she wants something he does not want, like children, then Seymour is there. The women have all been cover-girl pretty, but that's small compensation for the feelings of emptiness and loneliness that Seymour brought into therapy each week.

5. *Jane, 37*: Divorced, no children, Jane's a
    skilled architect. She's a health nut for
    whom no man shapes up. She's convinced
    all the "good men" are either married,
    emotionally unavailable, gay, or too old.

What is the common denominator in all five of
these cases? Feelings of inferiority. Each has a
deeply felt need for intimacy, but also a fear of
making mistakes or being rejected. Counseling
provided some progress by bringing out hidden
emotions and making evident certain habits or self-
defeating cycles of behavior. Often I'll combine
counseling with referrals for such things as body
work (also known as body therapy, which employs
various types of reflexology and massage
therapies). Exercise and meditation programs have
been useful too. Anything that puts these people
more in touch with themselves seemed to help them
deal more effectively with their feelings of
inferiority.

Masturbation: Sex with Someone You Love

For people currently without partners, the issue of sex
is a practical one. Let's assume you're a healthy, horny
single person. Perhaps you don't feel there's anything

wrong with having affairs or sex without intimacy. That's one way of solving the dilemma, providing that sex doesn't become exploitative or a hurtful arrangement. For most people, that's hard to do.

As novelist Barbara Kingsolver put it, "Sex is the ultimate animal necessity. We can't get rid of it." So one alternative is to masturbate. Most healthy, normal people do. To paraphrase Woody Allen on masturbation in *Annie Hall*, don't knock having sex with someone you love. Women in particular have expressed guilt or "feeling stupid" about masturbating. But many have come to feel more comfortable with it over time.

The crucial question for many people, however, is how much is too much? Once is too much if you don't like it, or if it's tiring or related to guilt. Any so-called "normal" activity, like eating or drinking, can become compulsive. So if you must have a compulsion, please choose masturbation. It's the least harmful, and it is cost effective.

Thoughts Are Not Harmful

There's no need for guilt about masturbation, nor is there any reason to feel guilty regarding your thoughts, dreams, and fantasies. These are normal, regardless of who or what they are about. It doesn't matter whether they concern your lover or your mother. If, however, you feel guilty about these thoughts or dreams, then they become problematic. You will experience them over and over again, because guilt is the energy for the repetition of unacceptable thoughts. (Obsessional thinking is not the same. It is a neurotic behavior usually involving repetitive preoccupations with irrelevant and absurd thoughts, which can render a person dysfunctional.) By themselves, thoughts are not harmful, but behavior can be.

Intimate Matters

The pinnacle of love is intimacy. In Erich Fromm's *The Art of Loving*, the author writes that intimacy thrives on four distinct qualities:

1. Caring deeply about your partner's welfare and growth.
2. Respecting your partner's identity—for their right to be who they are, rather than how you would like them to be.
3. Taking responsibility to care for the other person in an involved, active way.

4. Knowledge of the other person—his or her values, needs, wants, dreams, foibles—without which love may feel empty.

The (Intimate) Art of Listening

A great gift that lovers can give each other and that enhances the qualities of loving Fromm describes is the gift of listening. In our hectic, complex world, there often appears to be precious little time for or interest in listening. Listening to another involves quieting our own thoughts and concentrating on the message we are receiving. To be listened to is an act of intimacy. It's a process that communicates, "Your inner being is valued and important, please share it with me."

Since true intimacy represents a strong togetherness and a distinct separateness, a person should be able to say, "Whether either of us wishes to be alone or together, no threat exists." Intimacy thus becomes a delicate balance between dependence and independence, between giving and receiving. Intimacy suffers among individuals who fear the closeness that love might "impose" on them, as well as among those who fear solitude and cling desperately to their lover.

Commitment is ultimately required for intimacy to flourish. It also requires that we explore together the meaning of our feelings for the foreseeable future. Reluctance to open oneself up is understandable when it is uncertain whether next week or next month may bring an end to the relationship.

Real excitement and meaning between people is found in the quality of intimacy they share. Sexual techniques and experiences can contribute to intimacy, but they are only the "how-tos" in a mutually responsive relationship.

Perhaps the greatest value of the sexual revolution of the 1960s can be found in the dialogues it provoked in society concerning these issues. The revolution heightened people's awareness that dilemmas existed, opening the way for love and sexuality to be understood anew. The real "turn-on," in the parlance of that era, is intimacy.

In the February, 1997 issue of *The New Women*, Harriet Lerner said it well:

An intimate relationship is one in which we can be who we are (rather than what the other person wants and expects us to be) and allow the other person to do the same. This means we can say what we think and feel in a relatively uncensored way, and we can share both our competence and our vulnerability without having to hide or exaggerate either. Authenticity and truth-telling—and the sense of safety, ease, and comfort in a relationship that make these possible—are at the heart of intimacy. An intimate relationship enlarges—rather than diminishes—our sense of the world and ourselves.

Intimacy is greatly enhanced by what has come to be known as "differentiation," which is based on the assumption of the uniqueness of each human being. "Differentiation," as psychotherapist David Schnarch writes, "allows us to experience fully our biologically based drives for both emotional connection and individual self-direction. The more differentiated we are—the stronger our sense of self-definition and the better we can hold ourselves together during conflicts with our partners—the more intimacy we can tolerate with someone we love without fear of losing our sense of who we are as separate beings."

In finding your own voice, you become strong enough as an individual to increase the possibility of having an intimate, fulfilling, and lasting relationship the next time around.

Nonverbal Intimacies

Intimacy is a metaphor for the limitless verbal and nonverbal forms of communication that transpire between two people. Gazing into each other's eyes, holding hands, lying together in front of a fire, massaging or bathing each other, cooking favorite meals, or simply sensing each other's presence in a crowded room are a few of the many nonverbal intimacies that people exchange. Often, these gestures communicate more than any words can.

Shifting Balances in a Relationship

Intimate relationships create an atmosphere of tolerance for a partner's different moods and interests. In loving interactions, two people don't always feel the same. They can be loving and caring, for instance, or irritable and upset. There's a flow back and forth in which sometimes you are concerned for the other person more than for yourself. You are sensitive and responsive to the needs of your partner. Equilibrium is achieved not through a static balance in which things are always equal, but rather through a shifting imbalance in which first you care for a partner's needs, then you receive care in return. Sometimes you are active, and sometimes you are passive.

Timing in intimate relationships is also critical. This is especially true in the area of honesty. Lovers, spouses, and even friends often wonder how much they should tell about themselves, and when is a good time? Although honesty is often a good policy, there are cases when it can be wrong. Indeed, people sometimes regret having told the truth for good reasons. For example, a partner may not be ready, and may perceive being told a truth as a spiteful act. Whether it's done consciously or unconsciously, telling the truth can be a hostile act.

Before you potentially violate an intimate relationship, explore your motivation for confronting a partner with a sensitive truth. Is it appropriate to tell a partner about your past sexual liaisons? Will it cause a hurt that is unnecessary and that could have been avoided? Of course, if a partner has had a history of promiscuously engaging in unprotected sex, it's unlikely that true intimacy will have developed. (In such cases, however, a partner is morally obligated to tell a potentially unsuspecting partner that he or she is at risk.)

Sex and Love: Different Ingredients

Sexual relations combined with love make a great recipe, but sex alone doesn't reflect the health of a relationship, nor does it serve as a barometer of its success. Sexual intimacy occupies a very small amount of time in the average week. There's no relation between the number of times a couple has sex and the viability or strength of their bond. If sex is the most important part, chances are you're not communicating well about other, more vital aspects of your partnership. For instance, can you sense and empathize with each other's moods? Can you be comforting? Can you take care of each other without worrying about who did it last?

Intimacy Can Be Sex-Free

> *There's always something alarming about love, but friendship is forever our guardian angel.*
>
> —Owen Dodson

Sex, Intimacy, and Friendship

There's an assumption that committed couples cannot sustain intimate and caring friendships with the opposite sex. They can and do. The idea that an intimate relationship inevitably translates into a sexual affair is false. I have known many couples who have committed relationships where each partner has intimate friendships with either the same or opposite sex. Such deep and intimate friendships often strengthen and enrich the primary partnership.

Often in a good marriage or relationship, the couple characterizes each other as "best friends." In this context, another friend could also be called a best friend. If this is too confusing, then try using the phrase "my next-best friend."

People may feel threatened when a partner has a friend of the opposite sex. But in trusting, secure relationships, this is usually not the case. While sex is seen as a powerful force, it doesn't compare to our need to love and be loved.

Intimacy does not need or depend on sex. Too often I see couples locked in suffocating relationships in which a controlling jealousy hides as "caring." In such cases, neither partner grows. When a relationship is strong, we can avoid acting on feelings of love that, admittedly, can be generated by intimacy.

M. Scott Peck addressed this point in his book *A Road Less Traveled*:

> *I may meet a woman who strongly attracts me, whom I feel like loving, but because it would be destructive to my marriage to have an affair at that time, I will say vocally or in the silence of my heart, 'I feel like loving you, but I am not going to'. . . . True love is not a feeling by which we are overwhelmed. It is a committed, thoughtful decision.*

On Intimacy, Friendship, and Love

In *Love Undetectable*, a brilliant analysis of the history of friendship, Andrew Sullivan describes some advantages of friendship over romance and marriage. The attraction of romantic love, to paraphrase Sullivan, is that it can eclipse every other emotion and transport us to levels of bliss we've never felt before. Love seems eternal, which is why, Sullivan concludes, love is so irresistible and so delusory. The impossibility of love accounts partially for its attraction. "It is an irrational act, a concession to the passions . . . and in almost every regard, friendship delivers what love promises but fails to provide."

Love is often an issue of control and counter-control, but nothing could be more unlike friendship. A condition of friendship is the letting go of power over another. As soon as a friend attempts to control a friend, the friendship is finished. Abuse of power can end not only traditional friendships but also love relationships, which should have a true friendship at its center.

· 11 ·

Finding Your Own Voice

Here are some ideas on how to develop self-respect and self-esteem. If you do nothing for anyone else in your ordinary life, change it. Take a six-month vacation from yourself to find yourself. If you love children, become a volunteer at an emergency shelter. If you enjoy singing, join a choir. Help with administrative stuff, too. If politics gets your juices flowing, be active.

Other ideas to jump-start your new energetic self:

- Participate in a children's reading group at your local library.
- Visit the elderly at a local nursing home.
- If you hate to sit with a book, listen to them on tape.

- Exercise to get your endorphin levels up. (Endorphins are an energy-producing chemical the body produces naturally.)
- Join an environmental group.
- Go to concerts, movies, and museums.
- Learn how to play bridge, chess, or a musical instrument.
- Take adult education classes.
- Relax yourself by trying yoga, meditation, and massage.

In short, develop, investigate, and pursue a new interest that will put you in touch with the type of people you enjoy being with. If you are tired and disillusioned by generic single's dating groups, try those organized by special interest: music, book, poetry, or religious study groups.

While everything above applies equally to both genders, I'd especially encourage men to develop close friendships with other men. Often, men do not have anyone to talk to about the good and bad in their personal life. In one situation, a man isolated himself inside his failing marriage. Once his wife left him, he had no close male friends to talk to. Of course, one of the reasons for the failure of his marriage was that he had not developed enough of his own life outside the marriage—he had no voice of his own. He had no other life outside his wife and job. In short, he was not a very interesting person to be around for long periods, and his wife grew tired of his exhausting and empty attention, as well as the stultifying isolation of their lives.

In my experience, many men do not think they have the skills or time to talk to another man about personal situations. They do not think it's a *manly* thing to do. But it is a great way to enrich and strengthen one's emotional muscles. Make the time and you will develop the necessary skills. Join a men's group, possibly one at a church or synagogue (you don't even have to be a member there). Go for a beer with someone from work, or ask someone to go fishing or bowling.

Enhancing Your Life as a Single Person

It's a paradox. If you don't enhance your life as a single person, you may have a harder time finding a life partner. If you have already endured one or more failed relationships, you may continue on that road. Though you may be eager to find another partner, you'll have a better chance if you live life as a single person to the fullest. Living fully and enthusiastically *without a partner* is great preparation for finding the partner you want. You will feel stronger for having made this decision. You will feel in control of your life. You will gain the time and give yourself the freedom to discover who you are and what you want in life.

After a breakup, it's hard for us to get completely back into the here and now. We risk getting stuck in the past. We can't move back, and we can't move ahead either. The opposite of being stuck is living fully in the world, which means taking a rewarding journey of self-development. The opposite of being stuck is making the most of our opportunities and making choices. It means developing a clear vision of where we want to go.

If this is a tough, unquiet, or even sad period in your life, I understand it may be difficult to start or follow through on these suggested ideas. But changes will occur if you begin by:

- Not comparing yourself to other people
- Committing yourself to a meaningful goal, purpose, or cause
- Keeping Eleanor Roosevelt's insight close to heart: "No one can make you feel inferior without your consent."

- Reconnecting with old friends
- Revitalizing the friendships you now have
- Not being in a hurry about anything

How Will I Know If I'm Going in the Right Direction?

- You'll know when you are no longer tired all the time. You will have energy for the things you want to do.
- You won't be bored anymore. You will realize that if you were bored, you were boring to be with.
- You are not searching for THE meaning of life. You will discover that life is an opportunity for many meaningful experiences. *That* is the authentic meaning of life.
- You no longer need affirmation from others in order to feel valued.
- Bad thoughts no longer trouble you that much, only bad behavior does. You are no longer allowing the ghosts of your past to haunt you. You are being nicer and kinder to people.
- You still feel the need for revenge, but have decided that the best revenge is achieved by living well and being a better person.

- You will appreciate your own worth and value and have the strength to be accountable for yourself. You will also act responsibly toward others.
- You like yourself more in the presence of people you appreciate.
- You decide to find another partner by going on a free and joyous journey rather than to a predetermined destination.

· 12 ·

Where Are You Now?

Along the Road to Finding Your Own Voice

In exploring relationships prior to making a commitment, this book has been purposely designed so that your choice the next time around will be right for you.

Since I've been advocating the importance of finding your own voice to achieve a mutually rewarding and potentially lasting relationship, you may ask what you can expect when you do find it. For one thing, you'll increase your potential for finding a partner who is right for you. In finding your own voice, you will have the confidence not to agonize over what kind or how much love you feel. You will understand that love, however wonderful, is also volatile, confusing, and unreliable. You will have the strength not to use love as the sole criterion for making the crucial decision about commitment.

When you find your own voice, you will also be better prepared to make a commitment—whether you decide to live together or marry—by addressing these questions about a potential partnership:

- Do I really like this person?
- Can this person be a best friend to me?
- Does this person fully respect me?
- Would my desire for a measure of independence be compromised?
- Would we be able to deal with conflicts?
- Can I describe our relationship as comfortable and trusting?
- Do we have an open communication?
- Can each of us say easily about the other, "It makes me happy to see you happy."
- Do we enjoy pleasuring each other?

And, perhaps most important:

- In the presence of this special person, do I like myself more?

Is Your Partner "Teachable"? Can You Learn from Each Other?

Some people give up too soon with a new partner who does not meet certain standards. But consider this: Some men and women are actually "teachable." That is, if you tell your partner what turns you on or off, your partner will listen. She or he will integrate the information into his social, emotional, and sexual relationship with you. Whether or not you are "in love" with a partner is less important than an issue like this one.

Another crucial question is whether you can learn from each other. This is one of the most thrilling aspects of any relationship that continues to grow and thrive. If we are stuck with a rigid, unchanging, "I-always-have-to-be-right" partner, then it's no surprise when such a relationship becomes stagnant and dissolves. It is surely an unrewarding and unequal union, no matter how much security it seems to offer.

Regarding whether a partner is "teachable" or not, I'm not talking about asking someone to change his or her entire personality. If a partner is truly "teachable," she or he will be open to reaching out by changing or modifying certain rude, unattractive, or destructive behaviors. This willingness to change is a good sign that you may have found a worthwhile partner, one who is willing to listen to and share in the qualities of your own unique voice.

In finding your own voice, you will also be more equipped to spot the *wrong* partner when you:

- Meet someone who thinks almost exclusively in terms of "What's in it for me?"
- Are aware of feeling insecure when you're with this person
- Experience reawakened feelings of low self-esteem
- Meet someone who uses desperate messages of dependency that masquerade as love, such as "I can't live without you" and "Without you, my life won't amount to anything." (You will understand that such statements pose a very real threat to your autonomy.)

Here are a few indications that you are still far away from finding your own voice:

- You may feel tired most of the time
- You'll have a tendency to be mean, or easily angered over inconsequential and trivial things

- You betray yourself by unfavorably comparing yourself to others, or you disguise your insecurity by presenting a façade of arrogance and superiority
- You have a tendency to blame others for problems you have created and must solve yourself

Finding your own voice is empowering because:

- It means you are open to new ideas and experiences
- You will not remain victimized by traumatic and agonizing experiences of the past
- You are hopeful about the possibility of change
- You are not focused on comparing yourself to others
- It enables you to let go of feelings of unworthiness

Do you still have a way to go to find your own voice? That's okay. If you are not quite there, you are on your way if you:

- Begin to feel more energetic
- Pay attention to your health by experimenting with exercise programs, meditation, yoga, biofeedback, or massage

- Are into helping people by doing "mitz-vahs"—good deeds without any expectation of return
- Feel appreciated and good about doing good

Most important, you will feel confident and secure enough to be kind. I don't mean kind to everybody or under all circumstances. We are all only human. Unconditional kindness is unrealistic, perhaps even unnecessary. One can still be angry and upset by issues and incidents and still remain a basically kind and compassionate person.

Unconditional Love?

It's all right if you don't feel unconditional love for anyone. In my experience, it is an unrealistic concept. The responsibility of love, of caring for and respecting another individual, is not to be taken so lightly. Some people have asked me if loving God is the only channel through which we can love people. I don't think so. It's much easier to "love everybody" or to "love God" than it is to fully love one person.

A Very Special Kind of Therapy

Over the years, I've seen many people who over-came a poor sense of self-worth. By being the recipient of love from a good partner or by doing good deeds, they were able to achieve the self-assurance that was lacking in their lives.

In other cases, people were depressed after the death of a loved one or the breakup of a relationship. It was entirely healthy and appropriate for them to mourn, to be sad—for a time. But grief often lasts longer than a person can tolerate. When a lack of energy and loss of purpose pervade their lives, my intervention is something I call Mitzvah Therapy. "Mitzvah" is a Yiddish word meaning "a good deed." (In Hebrew, the word refers to rules in the Jewish orthodox faith.) The idea is to do good deeds *without any expectation of a return*. In its highest form, the deed is anonymous. Obviously, the return is feeling good about doing something worthwhile and helpful for another person or cause. It moves a person out of a preoccupation with his or her despair into helping someone else. The point is that you *can* help someone else, even when you feel as if you can't help yourself.

The process may be a gradual one. Sometimes a friend can help to get you started. A friend can research an appropriate volunteer placement and possibly even work beside you for a while. It is extraordinary how people have become transformed in response to this simple therapy. When someone appreciates you and values your help, it's like magic—better for most people in a few months than after a year on an analyst's couch!

Another key dimension of Mitzvah Therapy is to learn something new. When we learn a new thing, it moves us away from a preoccupation with sadness and self-pity toward something that offers us pleasure in achievement.

Ironically, I met a woman in Israel who could not grasp this relatively easy concept. I had spoken about Mitzvah Therapy on a popular morning talk show. That evening, a 60-year-old woman greeted me with, "You've got a lot of nerve singing the praises of Mitzvah Therapy. I've been doing mitzvahs all my life and I'm miserable!"

"You haven't been doing mitzvahs at all," I responded. "You expect gratitude or something in exchange for all the good work you do, like babysitting for your grandchild."

"How do you know?"

"Because you look tired. When you do anti-mitzvahs, or lay guilt trips on loved ones, it's exhausting. When you do authentic mitzvahs, it's energizing."

She stared at me a moment and said, "I think you're right." Then she left without saying another word. The brief exchange with this stranger ranks as one of the finest therapeutic moments of my long career.

Loving Yourself

Do you need to love yourself before you can love someone else? That's a common myth in the field of self-esteem. If it were true, it would doom millions of people to lifelong despair. For many, self-hatred is a fact of life. Sure, life is easier if you have high self-esteem, because your chances are better for attracting others. But if you don't like yourself, keep in mind that it's still possible to find someone who will. I've dealt with numerous people over the years who started out with a high degree of self-contempt. Yet how is it they were still able to dramatically change their lives for the better?

The following case history illustrates my point:

■ ■ ■ ■ ■

Sarah came from a family that did not appreciate or accept her. She did very well in school, but by the time she was a teenager, she was quite over-weight. Overeating was her best relief from stress. She was shy and had few social skills. She won a scholarship to a leading women's college, where she focused on her studies. She found herself friendless, dateless, lonely, and alienated from her family. After college, she entered government service as a research assistant. She also soon began a four-year period of psychoanalysis.

At age 38, Sarah was referred to me. Psychoanalysis, she said, offered no help. Although she did gain some insight into how her family affected her life, she described herself as being "more miserable than ever—overweight and unat-tractive." She felt hopeless about ever being able to find a partner. Her most common refrain was, "I hate myself; I hate my body."

Sarah came to me in a last desperate effort to improve her life. At this time, she was a high-level government employee with an excellent income. There was little point in treating her with conven-tional psychotherapy. I agreed to see her, but only if she accepted the following conditions:

1. We would meet once every two weeks.
2. She would go to a massage therapist twice a week.

3. She would take a one-hour daily walk.
4. She would do volunteer work at a center for neglected and abused children.

In a few weeks, it was apparent that Sarah was thrilled with what she described as her "new life." She was most surprised to find how effective massage therapy was. "He treats my body lovingly," she said. This was an entirely new experience for her. The children at the center adored her. They looked forward to her visits. Sarah felt needed and appreciated. "I've never been happier in my life."

If anything, she initially resisted the daily walks. She came to enjoy them as a refreshing way to decompress after work. (She was smart enough to realize that walking had represented an unwelcome public display.)

After two months, Sarah suddenly approached me with a smile. "Hey, Doc, I didn't want to tell you this, because I was sure that things wouldn't work out, and I would have to endure another disappointment. But the very first time I went to the children's center, I met a man who was also a volunteer. He was very friendly. I could see he was smart. He was also short, bald, and somewhat unattractive. We've become closer since that time.

He's still short and bald, but he's not unattractive anymore."

A year later, they married. Now, five years later, they are still a happy couple. (By the way, Sarah did not lose any weight. She was accepted as she was and as she is.)

■ ■ ■ ■ ■

Clearly, you don't have to start out by loving yourself in order to find the love that can transform your life. Sarah's story shows that although psychotherapy can open the door, it often is not the main reason for a person's transformation from low to high self-esteem. Chalk up another success for Mitzvah Therapy!

· 13 ·

Some Frequently Asked Questions About Relationships

What is meant by the concept of self-esteem?
I like the definition developed by the California Legislative Task Force on self-esteem in 1990: "Appreciating my own worth and importance and having the character to be accountable for myself and to act responsibly toward others." This is not the same as just feeling good about yourself. Some of the meanest people I know declare that they feel good about themselves, even while engaging in disgraceful behavior.

How do I know when I have found a real partner?
If you find someone with whom you share similar levels of respect, attention, honesty, trust,

and an emotional maturity to tolerate inevitable differences, then you have found your partner. It's still a good idea, however, to reread the chapter on "Before You Commit." Going into a serious relationship with your eyes open will give you a feeling of self-control and responsibility that can only make you a more sensitive partner. In a sense, you will have found your own voice, which will be energizing.

Does the changing family in America mean anything to my future relationships?

Yes. Better interpersonal relationships will create better families, slowing the frequency of marital breakdowns in America. Just being "in love" is not enough. Trust and respect must become equal to that volatile and undependable feeling.

Another point is that there's a growing acceptance of a variety of lifestyles. Therefore, your choice of a long-term commitment must be more thoughtful and serious than ever before. We are moving in the direction of the egalitarian family. That means we are seeing more families without children, without a marriage license, or comprised of same sex partners. More families come with foster, adopted, step- or grandchildren, and there are more single parents with children. There's a new spirit blooming, based on necessity and love, that respects everyone who is trying to create settings that benefit all family members. If you have children and are embarking on a new relationship, it's important to understand that the care and concern of loved ones is far more crucial than "doing all the right things."

I'm thinking of trying a traditional marriage for my second go-round. Are traditional roles in marriage dangerous to family life?

They can be. Violence is often seen as a by-product of a family life that stresses traditional roles, such as the authoritarian male and submissive female. In such unequal relationships, one partner is inevitably exploited. The frustration and anxiety generated by these forced roles has led to domestic violence and emotional abuse. In such cases, children can become innocent victims of suppressed rage.

You will be in a much healthier situation with a partner who agrees to share decisions about finances and vacations, who favors sharing chores, and who wants to share in the scheduling of activities for adults and children. Family equality makes both partners stronger, as well as offering positive role models for children.

I am over 40 years old and divorced. Will it be harder for me to find a new life partner?

There's an amazing statistic in Carmen Anthony's book *Getting Married after Forty*. Each year 275,000 Americans over 40 do remarry. Nevertheless, finding the right partner isn't easy at any age. But as a mature person, your odds of finding and keeping a partner may be higher than when you were younger. Young people who think that "being in love" is what matters most often find themselves ending up as one more divorce statistic. Good men—and women—have always been hard to find. Maybe we should focus on why we can't find "good" men and women. Maybe it's because we want *them* to be "good," absolving us from trying to become more like the kind of person we want to find. That's why finding your own voice is so crucial. Once you do, there will inevitably be a man or woman for you.

You can take comfort in this statement by the writer-director Peter Farrelly: "I didn't get married till I turned 40, three years ago. I think of all the women I fell in love with over the years whom I would have married if they'd only liked me. But thank God they didn't because I ended up with the perfect woman for me. Sometimes it's good not to get what you want."

I've tried very hard to find another partner after my divorce without any luck. What am I doing wrong?

Perhaps you are trying too hard. Take a six-month vacation from searching for a partner. Don't even think about it. Instead, go on a half-year journey of self-development. You can take tennis lessons, an art class, yoga—there are so many ways to go on a journey. If you can afford it, go on an actual journey to another country. Keep a journal of your meetings with people, your feelings and experiences. It pays to live optimistically. Live as though the partner you hope to meet will enter your life eventually.

Since my last relationship ended, I've been working extra-long hours and feeling too tired to even date. What can I do?

You may have fallen into the trap of a routine. If you have been working hard, no wonder you use the weekends to rest and recover. In such situations, people have told me they wish someone would enter their world, love them, and make the aching stop. Your tired and run-down feeling may be psychological in origin. This syndrome affects many people who say they "have nothing to look forward to." Do you feel unattractive or unworthy of happiness, or in some way inferior? Those could also be reasons you feel tired. Left unchecked, you may be turning these feelings into a self-fulfilling prophecy. Men and women like other men and women who like themselves. That doesn't mean they display an arrogance or ego that merely attempts to compensate for deep feelings of unworthiness and inferiority. It simply means "like." People who have self-respect and feel secure around others are usually fun to be with.

Can you give me examples of people who found their own voice and how it affected their lives?

Sure. Here are two of them.

1. Jane Fonda. Aside from the case studies mentioned earlier in this book, there's a fascinating interview with Jane Fonda in the July-August, 2000 issue of Oprah Winfrey's magazine, *O*. After three failed marriages with exceptionally high-powered men, she realized that she had always compromised herself to accommodate them. By doing this, she had lost her own voice, her own sense of self. "I want to not lose my voice again. And being by myself, that is to say, without a man . . . is allowing me to know what it feels like to live in my own skin and to remember what I miss and don't miss about

a relationship." One valuable insight was that "Sex and intimacy are not the same: you can have sex all your life and never be intimate with a person." It seems to me that her chances of choosing the right partner the next time around are far better.

2. Camryn Manheim. I recently visited Camryn Manheim, the 1998 Emmy winner for best supporting actress in *The Practice*, at her home. Her parents are among my oldest and closest friends. After reading Camryn's candid and inspiring memoir, *Wake Up, I'm Fat!*, I realized how pertinent her message was to my own book. Her success was based entirely on achieving a level of self-acceptance and finding her own voice.

She also won a Golden Globe award in 1999 and many other awards since then. I've known Camryn for years, and was delighted to see her self-acceptance and self-confidence on display when she proudly dedicated her Emmy to "All the fat girls!" But her success did not come easily. She was consistently told that "fat girls" don't make it in the acting business.

In 1993, Camryn wrote and starred in a brilliant one-woman off-Broadway show, *Wake Up, I'm Fat!* At one point, she tells the audience, "I'm not going to let my low self-esteem get the better of me." She endured difficult times dealing with family and cultural attitudes, as well as hard-on-herself feelings about her body image. "Sometimes I can't tell where I end and my fat begins," she said.

At one point in the show, she said, "Parents know how to push your buttons because they sew them on." The entire audience laughed and applauded at that line, and it was clear that Camryn had reached everyone. In her book, she worries whether people will care about "the hardships of being fat and feeling inadequate." She asks, "Would it resonate with anyone else?" She discovers that it does. "While all my life I had been saying to myself 'I suck because I'm fat,' others have been saying to themselves 'I suck because I'm short . . . I suck because I'm gay...I suck because I'm bald . . . I suck because I'm poor . . . I suck because I'm in a wheelchair . . . ' Ad infinitum. Everyone can find a reason to hate themselves, which they use as an excuse to keep themselves from moving forward. I sure had."

When she wasn't getting acting roles, Camryn learned sign language, becoming a fluent interpreter for the deaf. It was a major step toward self-acceptance. If you feel good about yourself, your positive presence will be felt around you.

Camryn will be fine whether she chooses to have a partner or not.

Final Thoughts on Your Quest for a Life Partner

How your quest for a partner progresses needs to be decided by you and you alone. No book or person is going to have the "right" answer for you. Whether you find a potential life partner through an Internet chat room, on a blind date, using a dating service, or just asking a friend at work out for coffee, these are all neutral acts. It is what happens *after* the initial meetings that can be significant in your life.

Be willing to seek what you believe you need in a partner. And, for goodness sake, don't take the process too seriously! And don't make someone else responsible for the result. Stay open to surprise in life. For the happiness you seek is potentially, perhaps when you least expect it, within your grasp.

· 14 ·

Epilogue:
Additional Relationship Facts
and Ideas

According to research cited by Kathleen Kelleher in *The Los Angeles Times* (September 18, 2000), the chance of a first marriage ending in divorce over a 40-year period is 67 percent. She adds: *"Half of all divorces occur in the first seven years of marriage."*

Things are changing. In today's world, you can feel freer to make choices in relationships. Here are a few facts and ideas to consider.

New data on cohabitation by the Institute of Social Research at the University of Michigan found that cohabitation both before and in lieu of marriage has become so commonplace that it is practically the norm. Fifty-six percent of all marriages between 1990 and 1994 were preceded by cohabitation. From 1965 to 1974, the figure was 10 percent (*New York Times*, February 15, 2000).

From a film review in the *New York Times* (March 16, 2000) of a documentary study of middle-aged swingers: "There's something courageous and healthy in their demonstration that you don't have to be young and beautiful to find sexual pleasure and celebrate the erotic."

Think about what Philip McGraw says in *Relationship Rescue* (Hyperion):

"Falling in love is not the same as being in love. Relationships are negotiated, and the negotiation doesn't ever end. The contract is that you are going to stay together, not that you are going to stay together exactly the way you started."

As the highly respected anthropologist Helen Fisher recently observed, American women engage in sex earlier, take more sex partners before marriage, live with partners outside of marriage, marry later, and divorce when spouses do not satisfy their needs.

Bride magazine reports that marriage today is a $70-billion dollar industry, with the average wedding costing $19,000. Elsewhere, research has suggested that the more costly the wedding, the less chance the marriage will last.

As a recent article in the *Herald Tribune* reported, even in a still largely male-dominated and conventional society as Japan, women are starting to put off marriage until much later ages.

Another *Herald Tribune* article reported that about 10½ million women in the United States earned more than their husbands in 1998.

"Nothing in my world, nothing in my self-definition," says Kevin Powell in "Confessions of a Recovering Misogynist" (*Ms.*, April–May, 2000), "prepared me for dealing with a woman as an equal."

Times *are* changing.

As some of the above ideas indicate, it has taken American society some thirty years to catch up to Nena and George O'Neill's brilliant 1972 work, *Open Marriage*. This is a work I especially recommend for people fed up with a conventional marriage. The least important message of the book is that sexual intimacy with another person could be acceptable within a strong and thriving marriage. Rather, the O'Neills focus on the idea that a good relationship is not possible without equality. They make a special point that the biological urge to mate has little or nothing to do with the roles that a given society ascribes to the male and female.

The book is still valid, despite the fact that the O'Neills' own marriage was not successful. What was once threatening to conventional society now seems like common sense. Here are a few paraphrases of how the O'Neills described the realistic expectations of an open marriage:

—You will share most but not everything.

—Each partner will change, which can occur through conflict or gradual evolvement.

—Each partner will accept responsibility for him- or herself.

—You cannot expect your partner to fulfill all your needs, or to do for you what you should be doing for yourself.

—Should you choose to have children, you will accept the role of parenting willingly as your greatest responsibility.

·Appendix A·

Recommended Reading

Angier, Natalie. *Woman—An Intimate Geography*. Houghton Mifflin, 1999.

Beck, Aaron T., M.D. *Love Is Never Enough*. Harper & Row, 1988.

Blau, Shawn. *The Albert Ellis Reader: A Guide to Well-Being Using Rational Emotive Behavior Therapy*. Carol Publishing Group, 1998.

Buber, Martin. *The Way of Men*. Citadel Press, 1950.

Buscaglia, Leo. *Living, Loving, and Learning*. Fawcett, 1983.

Carter, Steven and Julia Sokol. *Men Like Women Who Like Themselves*. Delacorte, 1996.

Cassell, Carol. *Swept Away: Why Women Fear Their Own Sexuality*. Fireside, 1989.

Dalai Lama, and Howard C. Cutler. *The Art of Happiness*. Riverhead Books, 1998.

Dodson, Betty. *Sex for One: The Joy of Self Loving*. Crown, 1987.

Ellis, Albert. *How to Stubbornly Refuse to Make Yourself Miserable about Anything—Yes, Anything*. Lyle Stuart, 1988.

Frankl, Viktor E. *Man's Search for Meaning*. Touchstone, 1984.

Fromm, Erich. *The Art of Loving*. Bantam, 1956.

Glasser, William. *A New Psychology of Personal Freedom*. HarperCollins, 1998.

Gordon, Sol. *A Friend in Need*. Prometheus Books, 2000.

Gordon, Sol, and Craig Snyder. *Personal Issues in Human Sexuality*, 2nd ed. Allyn & Bacon, 1989.

Gordon, Sol. *Raising a Child Responsibly in a Sexually Permissive World*, 2nd ed. Adams Media Corp., 2000.

———. *Why Love Is Not Enough*. Adams Media Corp., 1990.

Gottman, John. *The Seven Principles for Making Marriage Work*. Crown, 1999.

Hesse, Hermann. *Siddhartha*. Viking Penguin, 1999.

Jordan, Margaret and Paul Jordan. *Do I Have to Give Up Me to Be Loved by You?* Hazelden Foundation, 1994.

King, Rose. *Good Loving/Great Sex*. Random House, 1997.

Klein, Marty. *Ask Me Anything*. Pacifica Press, 1996.

———. *Your Sexual Secrets*. Berkeley Press, 1990.

Kundera, Milan. *Immortality*. HarperCollins, 1999.

Kurtz, Paul. *Exuberance*. Prometheus Books, 1985.

Lerner, Harriet. *The Dance of Intimacy*. Harper & Row, 1989.

Main, Darren J. *Spiritual Journeys along the Yellow Brick Road*. Findhorn Press, 1999.

Manheim, Camryn. *Wake Up, I'm Fat*. Broadway Books, 1999.

May, Rollo. *Love and Will*. Delta, 1989.

McNaught, Brian. *Now That I'm Out, What Do I Do?* St. Martin's Press, 1997.

Nelson, J. *Between Two Gardens—Reflections on Sexuality and Religious Experience*. Pilgrim Press, 1983.

O'Neil, Nena and George O'Neil. *Open Marriage*. Avon, 1973.

Peck, M. Scott. *The Road Less Traveled*. Arrow, 1990.

Pines, Ayala M. *Falling in Love: Why We Choose the Lovers We Choose*. Routledge, 1999.

Reiss, L. Ira, and Harriet M. Reiss. *Solving America's Sexual Crises*. Prometheus, 1997.

Schnarch, David. *Passionate Marriage*. Henry Holt, 1997.

Schwartz, Pepper. *Love Between Equals*. The Free Press, 1994.

Sullivan, Andrew. *Love Undetectable: Notes on Friendship, Sex, and Survival*. Alfred A. Knopf, 1998.

▪ Appendix B ▪

Additional Resources

Journey Toward Intimacy
Series Author: Jeanne Shaw, Ph.D.
    A Handbook for Couples
    A Handbook for Singles
    A Handbook for Lesbian Couples
    A Handbook for Gay Couples
    Couples Enrichment Institute
    P.O. Box 420114
    Atlanta, GA 30342–0114
    Fax Orders (404) 255–7439

Sex Information and Education Council of the
    United States (SIECUS)
    130 West 42nd Street
    Suite #350
    New York, NY 10036
    (212) 819–9770
    www.siecus.org

▪ Index ▪

Index

Index